HE CALLS ME
REDEEMED

HE CALLS ME
REDEEMED

Cover Design | Editing | Book Design and Typesetting
Enchanted Ink Publishing

ISBN: 979-8-9892498-2-4 (E-book)
ISBN: 979-8-9892498-1-7 (Paperback)
ISBN: 979-8-9892498-0-0 (Hardcover)

WWW.ARMANKAYMAKCIAN.COM

ETERNAL LIFE PUBLISHING

Dedication

I dedicate this book to my wife, my best friend, my partner in all things in life, Nicole, and to my three sons: Arman, Nikos, and my precious baby on the way. Whatever success I have, you four are part of it. The greatest inspiration in my life has been the joy and memories we've shared together as a family.

Arman, Nikos, and my youngest son, your love, courage, laughter, kindness, purity, childlike faith, and incredible inner strength have kept me warm at times when the world has felt so cold. Daily, I have thought and prayed about the men you will become, and I am overwhelmingly proud and wait in anticipation and thank God in advance for the incredible ways He will use you. I hope and pray this book will always remind you to build your lives on the one and only sure foundation that is our Lord Jesus and that you will forever look to Him in times of inexpressible joy, as well as times of unthinkable sadness and trial.

In years to come, I hope you'll read these words and know that Jesus, a handful of friends and family, your mother, and you, my three sons, were and are everything that ever meant anything to me. You are the ultimate gift any father could receive, and I'll spend my life thanking

God for you and trying to live up to the greatest responsibility I have been called to. Without question, you are my greatest accomplishment.

I want you to know you can accomplish anything you imagine as long as you commit it to the Lord. Jesus said, "But seek first the kingdom of God and His righteousness, and all these things will be added to you" (Matthew 6:33 English Standard Version). "Trust in the Lord with all your heart, and do not lean on your own understanding. In all your ways acknowledge Him, and He will make straight your paths" (Proverbs 3:5-6 ESV).

Here, in two words, I give you the sum total of everything I have learned about life and the best advice for any circumstance that may occur in it: trust God.

Love always,
Daddy

ARMAN KAYMAKCIAN

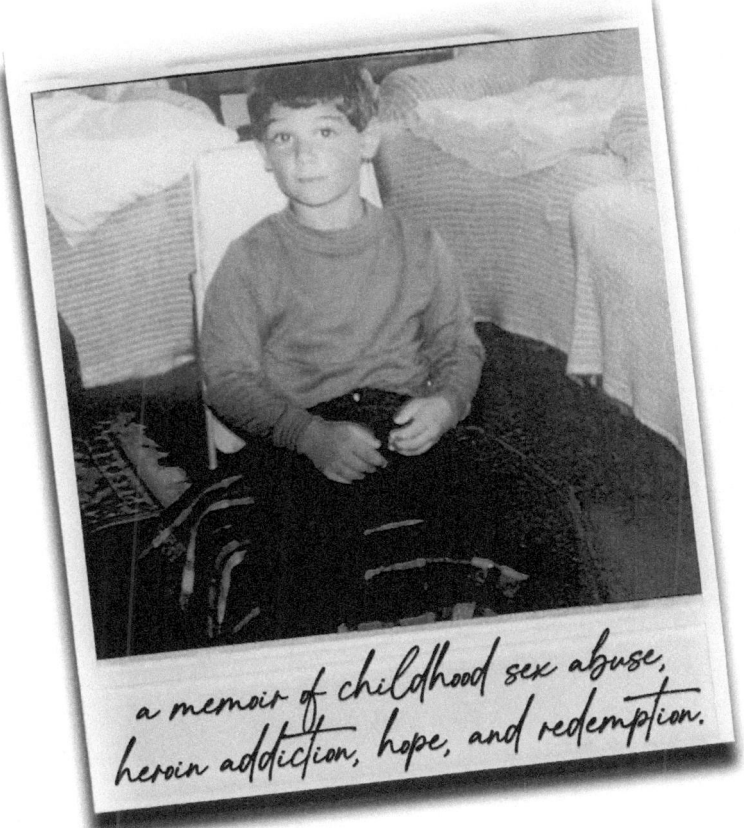

a memoir of childhood sex abuse, heroin addiction, hope, and redemption.

HE CALLS ME
REDEEMED

CONTENTS

He will redeem his soul from going down to the Pit,
And his life shall see the light.
Behold, God works all these things,
Twice, in fact, three times with a man,
To bring back his soul from the Pit,
That he may be enlightened with the light of life.

Job 33:28-30 New King James Version

INTRODUCTION

In 2010, I exited an NJ Transit train in Long Branch, New Jersey; it was the same train station I'd headed to a little more than a year earlier on my way to commit suicide. I was twenty-seven years old and starting my life over again, with all the odds you could think of stacked against me. I'd made a short list of accomplishments and goals for myself, and at the time, the list seemed impossible. I was a high school dropout who'd spent all of his adult life addicted to drugs. At the bottom of that list was more of an unattainable dream or wish rather than a goal, and that was to write a book about how Jesus had saved my life. Fourteen years later, God made it come to fruition, like so many other things that looked impossible back then.

Socrates said, "The unexamined life is not worth living." Examining my life and writing this book has been one of the hardest things I've ever done, and I offer it to you.

When I was a kid, I sometimes spent whole afternoons

wandering through the many empty rooms of my family's Armenian hotel in Asbury Park, New Jersey. I was all alone, and it was so quiet that at times the intensity of the quiet felt as if it were a sound. I studied the intricacies of those rooms—the furniture, the carpet, the imperfections in the moldings, the glass windows—running my hands over the fabric of the bedding, feeling different textures, taking special notice of paintings on the walls and their details and other objects, like ashtrays, small vases, bars of soap, and small amber-colored drinking glasses.

I don't know exactly why I did this, other than juvenile curiosity. It would have been impossible to do while the guests were there, but in the offseason—in the dead of winter, for example—the vacancy of the rooms allowed for it.

I've structured this book into sixteen rooms rather than chapters with the intention of walking together with you through the numbered doors of my memory, to which I alone hold the key. We will explore the perfect imperfections of my life, and it is my hope that my examination will inspire you to set off to search your own rooms. I'm about to tell you and show you things no one has ever seen or heard before. Many of them I didn't know myself before embarking on this journey.

Thank you so much for taking your time to listen and experience it all with me. Now, let's take a walk together through the memories I thought I had forgotten, which feel at times as though they were only dreams.

FIRST ROOM

SHOW ME YOUR SCARS,
AND I'LL SHOW YOU MINE

I LAY THERE ON THE GROUND, DISORIENTED, THE COOL crisp fall breeze rustling the colorful oak trees and brushing against the open cuts on my face and arms. My eyes settled on the bloody white-and-yellowish gravel with shards of glass lying on top. The small drifts of stone pebbles were smooth under my tiny fingertips, and I could smell the wood burning in people's fireplaces. I remember it smelled like Halloween. The taste of crumb cake was still in my mouth as I lifted my bloody arm into the air, reaching for help.

My sister, Michele, had been born with one leg shorter than the other, and after taking one look at me, she let out a horrified scream and did the best she could to limp quickly up the stairs of our small garage apartment.

My mother, a waitress, had been upstairs getting ready for work when it happened. She came running toward me and scooped me up in her arms, her thick dark Italian hair still partially undone, her white button-down shirt tucked into a black skirt and apron. The look of shock on her face filled me with dread. I was four years old and had no idea how bad my injury was. Her eyes bulged as she scrambled to figure out what had happened.

"Oh God, I can see his teeth, Daddy," my mother said frantically under her breath as my grandfather Tony came to see what had happened. The large bloody gash in my upper lip was open enough that my teeth were showing through it.

My sister and I had stood in the kitchen of my grandfather's house just a few minutes earlier. The house my grandfather and his brother shared was a sea of grainy mahogany wood and antique furniture and was decorated with little hand-carved wooden statues reminiscent of Nativity figurines imported from Italy and leftover Christmas decorations from the year before. Luciano Pavarotti's "Nessun Dorma" played faintly in the background while the smell of dust and Uncle Nick's pipe tobacco engulfed the entire house, a sweet-smelling aroma I still love even now. The lighting was dark in a way I appreciated, setting a dim ambiance throughout the house. I've always hated bright lights.

On the countertop, which was a strange mixture of mustard yellow and pale green with gold flecks sprinkled throughout, sat an unopened Entenmann's coffee cake in all its glory. We stood on the seventies linoleum, whispering to each other back and forth, arguing over which one would take the first slice even though we knew it wasn't supposed to be touched.

My sister handled the butter knife since she was six years older than me. Just as we took the first bite, the old rotary phone let out a god-awful ring so loud it caused my sister to drop her slice of cake and run toward the glass storm door. She shut it hard behind her as she ran out of the house. I followed quickly behind, slamming my hands into the glass with full force to push it open. With a loud smash, like something out of an action movie, I hit the glass and fell through.

Not long after, they wheeled me into the hospital while I screamed at the top of my lungs. My tiny arms and legs flailed as they strapped me to the stretcher with thick brown leather straps, which only added to my panic. I hated the feeling of the restraints. I couldn't stand being held down in any way; the lack of control was unbearable.

Bright fluorescent lights and novocaine numbed the sensations. I drifted in and out of consciousness. Brief images broke through of my mother's face and doctors in their gowns with faces covered by masks. They stood over me holding shiny metal instruments. The hospital had a distinct smell of excessive industrial sanitation. The pale green sheets, metal handrails, sharp institutional lines of tile, and clean paint surrounding me were unlike the jaggedness and charming imperfection of our little apartment and everything else in my world. It's as if hospitals, prisons, and schools are all speaking the same language. They all work hard to indoctrinate, to program, to control. I didn't realize it then the way I do now; I just knew how similar hospitals and school felt.

After I woke up from the anesthesia, I wondered where my father was.

"It's the best we can do," the doctor said.

My mother cried as she stared at the large gash in my upper lip, which was held together by stitches. "He's never gonna look the same! His beautiful little face . . ."

"We'll have to wait and see how it heals. It looks pretty clean," the plastic surgeon said.

"I know one thing—he'll never be able to grow a decent mustache; he'll always have a line right there in the middle," my father said unhappily.

It seems ridiculous now, but that comment absolutely shattered me. I would never be like my daddy, I thought to myself. My mustache would never look like his. How could I be a daddy if I couldn't grow a decent mustache like my own daddy? My mind raced around the anxiety from that statement, and it tangled me up inside, even as a four-year-old kid. Whenever I see the scar, I think about the weight of that comment my father made all those years ago—or at least the weight I thought it had in that moment.

Later, I lay on the purple-striped nylon couch in the tiny living room of our garage apartment at 365 West Park Avenue in Oakhurst, New Jersey. My parents were divorced, and I usually only saw my dad on the weekends. Though I had some pretty bad lacerations and was in a little pain, having everybody in our apartment at once was like heaven to me. I'd always loved having people around. I never wanted them to leave. I still don't. I love being alone, but I hate feeling alone.

My parents did their best to ignore their hatred for each other, being careful to be cordial in front of the visiting family as presents wrapped in all different colors and designs were offered up to me. I ripped them open one by one as I enjoyed my own personal Christmas morning in the fall. ThunderCats figures and My Pet Monster, followed by a Pogo Bal, Rocky workout cassette tape with tiny weights, and some other eighties kids' paraphernalia. Everyone *ooohed* and *ahhhed* as I opened the gifts. One of them, as I remember, was pretty lame: a children's book about different jobs, including a fireman, policeman, garbage man, and so on.

"What do you want to be when you grow up, buddy?" someone asked.

I looked around the room at the different faces, taking time to study each person as I thought about the question. It wasn't until my eyes landed on my father that my answer came to me. At first, I saw his feet—they looked just like mine—then his thick hands and fingernails—also just like mine. I paid careful attention to the scar on his right hand. He'd said it was from a burn made by his seam iron while installing carpet. It would be years and I would bear many of my own scars before I found out why he really had that scar.

"I want to be a daddy," I said, and they all went wild with laughter.

"A *daddy*?" They chuckled as they questioned me further, likely not because they were genuinely interested, but more so for their amusement—not that I blame them. Adults tend to lose their sense of freedom.

From the time we're toddlers, people begin to work on us, slowly chipping away at our ability to dream, to imagine, to play, to live intuitively. There's nothing greater than seeing a young boy or girl tie on a cape and jump off the furniture, believing in their heart they can truly fly. Some really simple yet profound statements have been uttered by the smallest of children.

I knew people worked for money, and I knew that working was important, but I wanted to be something more than just a worker. As I think about it now, my answer—that I wanted to be a daddy—was more of a series of unanswered questions than an answer. Like, where do we come from, and where are we going? What is our purpose? What was before us, and what will come after us? Why are we born, and why do we die? I was scared to die, and I was scared that my parents would die. I was scared to be alone on this earth without my dad. I wanted to be like him, because when I looked into his eyes, somehow, I saw my past and my future. I wanted to know what kind of man he was, what he was like, because I wanted to know what kind of man I would be. I knew God was a father, and I just figured that must be the most meaningful thing a person could be.

My father didn't laugh at my comment like everyone else in the room. Instead, he just smiled a big proud smile, picked me up, and hugged me.

"I want to be like you, Dad," I whispered as he patted my back.

"*Ayo, Janik,*" he whispered in Armenian. *Yes, my boy. God is gracious.*

He held me tight, his arms muscular with a single tattoo on his bicep—the old-world kind like a pirate might have, with a cross and a banner that read *RIP MOM*. My tiny cherublike face, with hazel-green eyes and long dark curly hair, pressed against his shoulder.

That kind of hug makes a person's heart stand still. It's the kind that makes you hold on a little bit longer and squeeze a little bit tighter, hoping to God it will never end, because they are never meant to end, but they always do. We would go on to hug each other many more times like that throughout my life, and it didn't matter how old I got or how life changed, those hugs still felt the same. My mind was set, and my goal was sure: One day I would hug my sons like that. I would be a daddy, and I would never let them go.

SECOND ROOM

Armenian Royal

THE ARMENIAN ROYAL HOTEL WAS A THREE-FLOOR, forty-two-room hotel just two blocks from the beach in Asbury Park, New Jersey, with an Armenian restaurant and dining room, complete with authentic Armenian cuisine, belly dancers, and live music. It was where I grew up and spent most of my summers as a kid.

I woke up in my room on the second floor, surrounded by light pine-paneled walls and an antique dresser with drip marks from when it had been repainted white. A small porcelain sink stood nearby, with just a little rustiness running down toward the drain from the slight drip that hypnotically put me to sleep on hot but breezy summer nights. The smell of the beach mixed with the floral notes of whatever detergent had been used to wash the thin hotel blankets. The toilet was walled off from the sink, next to the window, which was a pretty short distance from the house rented by a few Mexican families next door.

I walked across the navy blue carpet toward the toilet, pressing play on my tape recorder on the way. "In the Ghetto" by Elvis Presley played quietly as I stood there, my eyes still half-closed while I tried to aim. The cool breeze kissed my skin through the cracked window just before a loud bang resounded against the glass. I jumped and peed outside the toilet. A bird had flown right into the window, then struggled to fly away, stunned.

Fully awake after the bird's mishap, I cleaned up the floor and washed my hands with a cheap yellowish bar of soap, then splashed cold water on my face. That was something my father did every morning to wake himself up and a practice he'd taught me to do as well. I gave myself a look in the mirror, then got dressed to go downstairs.

A bunch of old Armenian ladies could always be found sitting on the front porch, talking about all types of subjects or playing cards for pocket change they reluctantly dug out of beat-up olive-green or mustard-yellow leather purses with their wrinkly hands. The old ladies had names like Gayane, Araxi, Mari, and Lucí.

The porch was a pretty large area, walled halfway up, with white columns holding up the roof above. There was a spiderweb in the corner that Uncle Jirayir (who I called Uncle Elvis) and I would throw small insects into so we could watch the large resident spider hunt and wrap its prey. In the front yard stood a tall yellow sign with red letters that read *Armenian Royal Hotel*, with a small crack right above the word *Armenian* from the time I'd tried to kick a football over the top of the sign like a field goal.

A number of tables and chairs were situated atop the dark blue carpet. The most popular of those was a round wooden table that belonged to the old ladies. A fluorescent light hung above it, which allowed card games and the action of the low-income housing across the street, called the Breakwater, to go late into the night. On most nights and especially weekends, the Breakwater had constant police activity and domestic situations.

I walked out onto the porch. The ladies always got excited when I appeared.

"Oh! *Bari loois! Iskhan eh, artuni!*" *Good morning! The prince is awake!*

A couple of them patted an empty seat for me at their table.

"Did you pray yet this morning, *anushik*?"

"*Ayo.*" I nodded and kissed the golden cross around my neck, impressing them by making the sign of the cross in Armenian, which they followed along with, moving their mouths and hands.

"*Anun hor yevort Vor, yevort Kooyn, Soorbo.* Amen." *In the name of the Father, and of the Son, and of the Holy Spirit. Amen.*

"*Abres!*" *Attaboy!* They took turns pinching my cheeks until a few police officers walked up to the steps.

"Good morning, ladies," one officer said.

Lucí's eyes became wide and terrified as she looked at the badges and weapons that accompanied their neatly tailored uniforms. She quickly grabbed both of my shoulders with her frail wrinkly hands and shuttled me through the front door. My father came walking toward us from the dining room. He wore a black tank top, his skin tanned. He was strong back then, in his early thirties and muscular, sweating and out of breath from his morning workout. He was good-looking, with gentle brown eyes, full lips, and a tiny space between his two front teeth. His complexion and hair were lighter than the rest of my family's, more reminiscent of his mother, Mari, who had passed away when he was twelve while giving birth to his little sister, also named Mari, though my father called her Biggie. No one knows exactly why, since she's as beautiful and slender as they come.

My father's name was Manuk, which means *baby* in Armenian, but a lot of people called him Mike or sometimes Manny. Everyone in my family had multiple names and identities, constantly shifting between White, Black, and Armenian cultures, doing business with the lower, middle, and upper classes, making connections wherever we could. We had Armenian and English versions of our names. For example, Uncle Arax was called Alex or A-Rax so people could dismiss the soft *ahhh* sound and replace it with the harsh American English long A sound that destroys the poetic pronunciation of almost every Armenian name, including the Arax, the river in Armenia after which he was named.

My name is Arman. I was named after my grandfather Arman, whose real name is Ermiayis, but many people call me Aj or sometimes Armin, which rolls off the tongue the way people say Arm & Hammer (or *Armin* Hammer) baking soda, which I hated as a kid. The only worse butchery of proper pronunciation I can think of is when someone will say, "Oh, so you're *Armanian*? Where is *Armania*, anyway?" To which I always want to reply, "Beats me, but *Armeeeenia* is to the east of Turkey, to the west of Russia, and above Iran." But I never do, for fear of hearing the person pronounce Iran as *Eye-ran*.

My brother, Raphael, we all called Raphi, which somehow morphed into Ralphi. Some of us even have extra names, like Uncle Jirayir, who people call Jerry. Some people, including me, called him Elvis. One time when I was walking with him through Queens, New York, in the eighties, some Columbian gangsters called him Ricky, a name my father made fun of by calling him Ricky Ricardo. "He wishes he were Spanish," my father would say while he rolled his eyes and made a goofy face.

Maybe we had so many names because it wasn't easy to live in a post–Armenian genocide world, even a few generations later, so far away from our roots. Maybe we needed to be all things to all people in order to survive and carve out a little piece of the American Dream. Either way, I think it comes naturally for us to adapt anywhere we land on God's green earth since we are a people the Turks and Azeris have historically had a unique genocidal intention to erase from history, geography, and memory. Even as I write this in 2023, we are global citizens; we not only survive but thrive wherever we live. And at times, my father made surviving look effortless. At others, he made it look harder than it should've been.

"Manuk! *Gendarmes! Gendarmes! Durs eh!*" Lucí said. *Police! Police! Outside!* "*Haydeh! Haydeh!*" *Quick! Quick!* "Hide him!"

"Okay, *hokis.*" *Hokis* means *my soul*, a term of endearment. "*Gamats, gamats, honkist.*" *Relax, relax, sit down.* "You wait here," my father said as he sat us down on a couch next to one of the fireplaces.

Lucí had survived the Armenian genocide of 1915. Her parents were taken by the gendarmes, or Turkish police, in the middle of the night and later murdered during a death march toward Deir ez-Zor, Syria. Lucí and her older sister escaped. Now eighty years old, she sat there with me on the couch in the lobby of our hotel, crying, praying, and petrified of two local Asbury Park police officers who were asking some general questions about who knew what. She had suffered a trauma so incredibly horrific that she was living though it again some seventy-five years later a world away from Turkey in a state called New Jersey.

I didn't know a whole lot about the genocide at that age. I was only eight years old. I do recall trying to do a report in school and finding only one page of information about Armenia in the encyclopedia in the library. Needless to say, it wasn't much help in understanding our history, but there was about half a page about the genocide in 1915, and when I read it, my mind made the connection to the time a wealthy Turkish family had visited the hotel. They'd called us something: *Ermeni kopecki. Armenian dogs.* "If we were in Turkey now, they'd be kissing our feet, but here, they're brave," they'd said as they laughed. It was said under their breath after a dispute over the food they had ordered.

My father was a bold man. He never took any nonsense from anyone and forcefully threw them out in the middle of their dinner. My grandfather Arman, who owned the hotel, was furious with my father until he learned what the Turkish man had said. After that, he was quiet for a minute, and then his eyes became squinty like they always did when he was angry. I knew that look well because whenever I did something that annoyed him, I would get that same look, only two inches away from my face, accompanied by his heavy Turkish Armenian accent asking, "Arrr you loooking in my eyes, misterrrr, ehhhh?"

Those same old squinty eyes settled on my father, and then he said, "Good! Good for you, *chojukus! Siktir!*" *Get lost!* he said in Turkish.

I was aware that my grandfather was from Beşiktaş, Istanbul, Turkey. He was what we Armenians refer to as *Bolsa Hye*, meaning Armenians from Bolis, short for Constantinople—in other words, Turkish Armenian. And I knew we had many Turkish friends and mixed Turkish words in with our Armenian language. I'd heard Turkish music play at our hotel. Our chef, Ali, was from Turkey, and I loved Turkish food. Still, I could sense that the relationship between Armenians and Turks was long and beyond complicated. As I think of it now all these years later, I don't believe the hatred many Turks feel toward Armenians is as abstract or difficult to grasp as I once thought; I just think for the Turks, the denial of the Armenian genocide has become as much or more a part of their identity and sense of belonging as the fight for recognition and justice for that same genocide—which is denied year after year—has become a part of ours as Armenians. This denial and lack of accountability has ultimately led once again to a modern day genocidal attempt of the Armenian people, in plain sight of the world at the hands of Azerbaijan.

I felt bad for Lucí as I sat there with her and wondered how people could hate us so much that they would try to kill us—worse, *exterminate* us, as one old lady had told me. "Exterminate?" I'd asked. "Like bugs?"

Her eyes got small and beady, and she said, "Never trust a Turk, no matter how nice they seem, *chojukus*"—*my child*—"because the farmer pets the hen with his left hand and steals her eggs with the right. *Haskatsar?*" *Understand?*

Still, I was sure there were trustworthy Turks and untrustworthy ones, just like every other group of people.

Sitting there with Lucí, I think it may have been the first time I truly understood that while I was an American boy who spoke the language most Americans spoke, liked all the American things American boys liked, watched American TV, enjoyed American food, listened to American music, read American comics, traded American sports cards, enjoyed Fourth of July fireworks and waved American flags, was and am very proud to be an American—to have been born and raised in and to be a product of America—I was also a boy of Armenian lineage, from a very long arduous Armenian history. I had an Armenian father, Armenian grandparents, and Armenian aunts and uncles. I lived in an Armenian hotel with an Armenian restaurant, ate Armenian food made by Armenian hands with Armenian-colored skin, liked Armenian shish kebab pierced with Armenian skewers, cooked over an Armenian grill with charcoal—the traditional Armenian way—accompanied by

Armenian rice pilaf. I watched the adults drink Armenian liquor, called raki or arak, from small glasses or Armenian coffee from Armenian demitasse cups and flip them upside down to listen to Armenian fortunes being told by old Armenian ladies sitting in chairs that were of Armenian design. I was surrounded by Armenian paintings of majestic snowcapped Armenian mountains and was accustomed to live Armenian music played by Armenian musicians, like my father, with Armenian instruments. I knew Armenian belly dancers with Armenian bells attached to their fingers, clanging together and sounding very . . . yup, you guessed it: Armenian. I watched my grandfather, who was always dressed in a suit in his Armenian way, celebrating with Armenian friends, doing Armenian dances, singing and snapping their fingers, retelling Armenian stories told to them by Armenian ancestors about Armenian heroes, and telling me to be proud that I was Armenian. They laughed at Armenian jokes while I snuck into the kitchen in our very Armenian hotel to steal rose scented Armenian rice pudding from the fridge.

I realized, whether I fully understood my identity yet or not, that I was just like my family—different in a special way. A different kind of American, one whose American spirit was very much integrated with a collection of ancient customs and symbolism, the significance of which I wasn't yet quite able to grasp. I didn't speak much Armenian, but I loved the way the words sounded. I liked the magic of the way the strange sounds ruminated in the back of the throat and rolled off tongues.

Geghetsig. Beautiful.

I loved making the rolling G sound. *Gh. Ge-ghe-tsig.* I found myself repeating it over and over again until I got it perfect. I thought of the Armenian words I knew and put them together with the word *beautiful*, adding the sound *eh* at the end, making it an absolute fact.

Aghchig ner gehetsig eh. Girls are beautiful.

Yerkink geghetsig eh. The sky is beautiful.

Giank geghetsig eh. Life is beautiful.

THE OTHER KIDS STAYING AT the hotel and I played a lot of games: hide-and-go-seek, which could last a long time in a forty-two-room building; Battleship, which mostly the boys played; or Monopoly or other board games on quiet afternoons when we weren't at the beach. But Amy Rodgers came up with the best game. It was a game of pretend that went like this: I would pretend to be the manager of the hotel and stand behind the front counter in the lobby, and she would walk in through the front door pretending to be a guest. Amy was two years older than me, skinny with dark blond hair, fair skin, light freckles, and blue eyes. She would ask me if there were any available rooms, and I would turn to the cubicles behind me that held the keys with diamond-shaped tags numbered for each room. I would hand her a key and tell her I would be up to check on her shortly to see if she needed anything.

Usually, she would answer the door and ask for towels or extra soap as part of the game, but on one particular day, it became the greatest game I'd ever played. She opened the door, grabbed me by my blue polo shirt, and pulled me into a room on the first floor halfway down the hall. Most everyone was at the beach.

We lay together on the bed, looking up at the white tin ceiling, our nervous breaths audible in the quiet. Butterflies flew around in my stomach, and I could sense they were aloft in her stomach too. I lay there with her, feeling like something intense was about to happen, and a split second later, Amy rolled over on top of me. Her body, though she was older, was smaller than mine, and she felt weightless. We started to kiss, and then we kissed, and we kissed, and we kissed. We could have kissed all day and all night. She kissed my neck, and I kissed her face and nibbled on her ear. She made noises and whispered. Her face felt soft against mine, and her skin smelled sweet. Her hair smelled of fresh shampoo. Her breath smelled and tasted like fruit-flavored bubble gum.

My body was totally relaxed, lulled by Amy, and every move our bodies made came effortlessly, naturally. I loved the way it felt to hold her and be held by her. We kissed for what seemed like a long time, though it was probably only a few minutes. After we finished our make-out session, she draped her leg and arm across my body, rubbing her foot back and forth on me, and nestled her head against my chest. We fell asleep like that until it was time to go downstairs for dinner. We exchanged smiles across the dining room, and it made me feel good.

It was a hot summer night, and my father and I decided to sleep on the roof to enjoy the stars and the beautiful breeze that God carried two blocks over from the ocean— our version of a camping trip on the Jersey Shore. As we lay there and talked, I had a goofy smile on my face that prompted my father to ask what I was so happy about. I never kept a secret from my father; he was my best friend in the world, and I knew I could tell him anything.

"I kissed her, Dad," I said, my face now becoming red.

My father sat up. "Kissed *who*?"

"Amy. We played this game and—"

"Oh, Casanova!"

"Dad! Stop!"

"Well, buddy . . ." He cleared his throat and scratched his head. "Just kissing, right?"

"Yeah, Dad. Just kissing. Boys are supposed to kiss girls, *cheh*?" *No?*

"Yes, that's natural, *yavrik*. Plus, you're a handsome little guy. No wonder she likes you," he said. "*Aferim.*" *Good job.* He chuckled.

I felt proud telling my dad about what had happened, and Amy and I made out every chance we got that summer of 1992. Just kissing.

THE THIRD FLOOR OF THE hotel was often left unoccupied. There was a haunted feeling up there and an eerie quietness to it. It felt so separate from the rest of the building. The colors were different, the carpet in the hallways blue rather than burgundy like the other floors. At the end of the hallway was a transparent white curtain that would blow around wildly from the wind, looking like a ghost bent on chasing me.

Sometimes, during the day, I would walk around looking inside the rooms and closets for something, though I didn't know what. I'd frequent my father's old room, the one that had been his after his mom died, when he moved from his tight-knit Armenian community in Montreal to an all-Black high school in Asbury Park. A yellowish-orangey-tan carpet covered the floors and the walls, and on the dresser sat a picture of my uncle Pete, who I'd never met. I knew he'd died when my father was young. I also knew it wasn't to be talked about. He'd been shot or something, and he was an artist; that's all I knew. In the photo, he wore a tuxedo and was clean-shaven. With his dark mustache, he looked like a mixture of my other uncles and my father—a variation of Kaymakcian features that was mysteriously foreign to me, though he shared more of my father's look than my uncles'. It would be years until I learned the story behind his death and what relevance it had to the scar on my father's hand.

There was another room that fascinated me. It was the last room on the left if you were facing the front of the building, the room where my father and Uncle Elvis would hide under the bed when the police came looking for them.

My father had told me, "If police come looking for me or one of your uncles or anyone else you love, you tell them you haven't seen us and that you're here alone with your stepmother. We will be hiding under the bed on the third floor in the last room on the left. They will not be able to find me, but you will know where I am, so you don't be worried, *haskatsar*?"

They did come looking, and they did ask me questions. I learned to be polite and respectful but to say very little. My father was always respectful and polite to the police, and though he mistrusted most of them, he taught me to always respect them and explained that they did a lot of good things.

One time when I was a small boy, they came in the middle of the night, and a group of them walked my father away in handcuffs. Dressed in black shorts with a globe on them and no shirt on, and his hands behind his back. He was still calm and respectful. He asked them if he could please put a shirt on, and they said no, pushing him forward, walking him past me in the lobby while I cried. I didn't understand and didn't really care about the details; all I remember is that they came in the night with guns to take my father away, leaving me sitting there wondering if he'd ever come back. From then on, it didn't matter what they asked. *Who is so-and-so? When was the last time he was here? Who is he to you?* I knew they were under the bed in the last room on the left on the third floor, but I didn't say so.

After the gendarmes had left, it was my job to go up three floors to that room and whisper *"Inkzinkeetbayeh,"* a phrase that means something like, *Keep it between us.* I wondered what made my father choose to hide under the bed and what he must have felt under there, until one day, he spoke about the day his mother had died.

My father looked like my grandmother, with light brown hair, gold-brown eyes, and a tiny space between their teeth. She was his best friend, and they were inseparable. Family photos have shown me my father the way he was at the age of twelve and my grandmother the way she was before she died. I can picture my father as a small boy, pulling on his mother's apron while she baked in the kitchen. I can see her sitting at the piano, playing a tune as my father sat next to her.

My grandmother died suddenly and unexpectedly, and time stood still for my father after that. He was never the same. After she passed, my grandfather was scared, angry, hurt, lost, and confused, and my father and his brothers would get beaten for minor transgressions. My father would hide under the bed to avoid the beatings. I imagine him as a young boy—scared, angry, hurt, lost, and confused—hiding from his dad under his bed, and I can see that as a grown man he was hiding under the bed on the third floor, out of breath, still somehow that twelve-year-old boy who'd lost his mom, never quite able to grow up, with too much of Mommy's lost little boy in him.

I would later find myself lost. Life paused at the age of ten underneath that same bed on the third floor in the last room on the left, when I was out of breath after running across Asbury Park from the gendarmes to the only place I'd be safe. I waited there, my heart beating fast, and listened carefully for my father's voice to whisper, "*Inkzinkeetbayeh.*"

THIRD ROOM

THE DOWNWARD SPIRAL

T HE SUN SHINED BRIGHT ON OUR QUIET NEIGHBOR-
hood in Long Branch, New Jersey, on Airsdale Avenue that summer of 1992. I put on a Bugs Bunny T-shirt
and cutoff jean shorts, laced up my Converse sneakers, and
looked out the window of my room. My friends played
baseball in the front yard, waiting for me to come downstairs. I threw a blanket over the black Japanese futon with
ancient-looking script that climbed like insects up the top
right corner. It had been given to me by Grandfather Tony.
"A futon made for a strong back," he told me. "Those Japanese have spines like iron." I made sure the Victoria's Secret
catalogs were hidden underneath the mattress before I left
the room.

I cringed at the sight of my mother's bedroom door as
I imagined what might be happening on the other side. My
sister, Michele, who was now sixteen, didn't seem to mind
my mother's boyfriend, Albert, moving in, or at least not in
the same way I did. The general uneasiness I felt was made

worse by the weird porn videos my friends and I had found in their room.

There was a cardboard box that Albert had found at a job while working as a plumber. One of the videos was S and M, with whips, strange piercings, and metal chains connecting body parts. We watched curiously, our little minds trying to make sense of what we were seeing, which was very unlike the *Playboys* my grandfather gave us a few years later, when we became more curious about the female form in all its glory, or the women's fashion catalogs we took from our mothers' mailboxes.

Those videos felt wrong and repulsed us. Some kind of law written on our hearts told us they were evil, a perversion of something that was meant to be good, yet we found ourselves unable to look away. I was later grateful to hear my mother express her disgust with those videos behind closed doors, to which Albert replied that he agreed, totally unaware that I had seen them or knew anything about them at all. It was a relief to know both Albert and my mother felt the same way about those strange videos that I did.

I made my way downstairs, feeling invisible and second place to the new man in our house. I imagined beating him off of her with a wooden baseball bat. It wasn't that Albert wasn't generally a nice guy, or that he wasn't good to me. But I was a frustrated ten-year-old boy who wanted my dad more than two days a week and wished it were him there instead.

I peeked at the homemade strawberry shortcake in the fridge that read *Happy Birthday, Aj!* with a number ten. A bowl of ambrosia sat next to it, with fresh green grapes, mandarin oranges, tiny white marshmallows, and shredded coconut. My mouth puckered at the sourness of the grapes, even while looking at it through the plastic seal I wasn't supposed to break. It was and still is one of my favorite desserts, made every year for a long time, though I haven't tasted it in almost a decade. I had read somewhere that ambrosia was eaten by the gods in some Greek myth, and I liked the idea of eating the food of the gods.

We had time before the party started, and my friends and I hopped on our bikes to head toward an overgrown grassy field just down the street, where we caught tiny frogs we called "penny frogs" by the dozens or an occasional garter snake. The birthday gift I had fantasies about that year was a chrome Mongoose BMX bike with black mag rims, matching chrome pegs on the front and back, and handlebars that could spin completely around in a 360-degree motion, which I had mostly put out of my mind since it cost almost $400. Four hundred might as well have been four thousand, especially in the early nineties.

A few weeks earlier, I had been riding bikes with a few kids when I spotted what looked to me like a chrome bike frame someone had tossed in the garbage. I slammed on my breaks and went to get a closer look. Small chrome spots underneath larger sections of gritty brown rust stood out in the summer sun like glimmering sterling silver or white gold or polished platinum. My eyes widened like I'd found a prized sapphire or diamond set in precious metal.

"Yo, that's junk, bro! Leave it," my friend Chris had said, out of breath from the bike ride. Sweat beaded up on his chocolate-brown skin and short curly waves of hair.

"Yeah, bro, it's just a rusty piece of junk," Eddie added in agreement. He was a few inches shorter than us, pale, and husky, and ended the comment with a corny chuckle as always.

"Nah, man, look at it! That's a BMX. Just gotta be cleaned up a little, that's all. Look at the chrome!" I said, trying to convince myself more than them.

It's hard enough to have a vision of something you think might be impossible without other people reminding you it probably *is* impossible. It had no wheels or chain or seat. It was, for all intents and purposes, useless. I picked it up and carried it away with my right hand over my shoulder, being careful to steer with the left hand during the ride a mile or so back home. I rushed into the house and slammed the door behind me, scaring our cat, Tony, who looked like a miniature lion, complete with a mane. He was a stray orange-striped calico with serious-looking eyes. I'd named him after my grandfather because he looked to me as if he had an old soul. I imagined that if he were a person, he would have been a seventy-year-old Italian man, so Tony made sense.

I rummaged through the cleaning products under the sink.

"Aj? What are you looking for?" my mother asked.

"Brillo pads, Mom! I found the greatest thing. It's out front. Come on, come look!"

There it stood, an old rusty bike frame flipped upside down on our front concrete walkway.

"Oh, Aj, that's garbage! Your bike is so much nicer. Throw that out!"

"No, Mom. It's gonna be great!" I tried to ignore the consensus of negativity between her and my buddies.

As she shook her head, part of me wanted to give in and not bother, but the other part of me became righteously indignant and even more determined to prove them all wrong and do something they considered impossible. I'd never considered anything to be impossible, not really, so I started in, scrubbing hard with a Brillo pad as my friends made fun of me. The loose steel strands from the Brillo stabbed my fingers and built up a steady blue film all over my hands and the entire bike. The chrome became shinier and more abundant as I scrubbed. I scrubbed and scrubbed some more, then rinsed it with water before drying it with a few rolls of paper towels I'd taken from Mom's kitchen. She smiled as I took another roll, and I nervously smiled back with a big cheesy grin. She watched me excitedly repeat the process two more times until every part of the bike frame sparkled like white gold at my grandfather's jewelry store in the Diamond District on Forty-Seventh Street in Manhattan.

Next, I walked down the street to Eddie's house. His father's garage was filled with bike frames, wheels, rims, tools, and other random bike and car parts. I bought a set of mag wheels, tubes, tires, a seat, and a bike chain with money from my room and hurried back to my house.

After a few hours, I'd finished installing the wheels, seat, and chain. I rode fast through my neighborhood in triumph, the wind in my face, feeling the sweetness of victory. My friends begged me to let them ride my repurposed trash. My mother hollered at me to be careful since it had no brakes as I hopped over the ramps we'd made from old plywood and cinder blocks. Breaks, I found, weren't really necessary. Instead, I stopped by rubbing the rubber off my sneakers. I rode until the streetlights came on after the sun had faded.

I went to sleep that night grateful for the bike, grateful I'd been able to see past what everyone else had seen, grateful I was nearly ten, grateful for my life, grateful for the Victoria's Secret catalog under my mattress—just grateful. They'd seen garbage, a useless irredeemable no-good piece of trash. But I'd seen treasure, and I'd worked hard to make my vision a reality.

As I think about it all these years later, I wonder if God looked at me—if He looks at us—like I looked at that bike that day. Maybe we're all just shiny bike frames accumulating rust as we go, the decisions we make or things that happen slowly corroding, destroying, oxidizing. Maybe we all just need a specific kind of Brillo pad.

While I slept that night, someone snuck into the backyard of our house and left with my bike. I cried looking at the empty space where I'd parked it. Little did I know, my father had worked out a payment plan with the bike shop owner to pay twenty-five dollars a week for nearly three months to buy the Mongoose I wanted for my birthday. I've imagined him getting off a carpet job on Friday afternoon, the sweat and carpet fibers burning his eyes, his knees sore from the kicker as he drove in that beige Ford van filled with scraps of carpet, multicolored padding, wooden strips with nails that poked his fingers, and double-sided surgical razors that occasionally sliced into his hands to the bike shop to make a payment of twenty-five dollars and telling the owner, "I'll be back next week with twenty-five more." I imagine he was thinking about my face and how I'd react when I finally saw the bike.

I can still see him pulling it out of the back of that old Ford van. "Happy birthday, buddy," he said. A hug and a kiss, and I was off.

The day of my birthday party, my mother's best friend, who I called Aunt Danielle, sat waiting for her boyfriend to arrive. He pulled up late in a black sports car and parked in front of our house just as one of my friends took a good crack at the baseball. As the ball headed toward the car, I recoiled, waiting for the inevitable thud. It hit the passenger door. He got out, slammed his door, and threw the ball down the street, screaming and cursing.

"I'm sorry, Rich! I'm sorry!" I called as he mumbled a few other choice words under his breath and shook his head.

Danielle came running over to calm him down. Eventually, he came inside, and we had cake. The grown-ups drank coffee, and I finally got to have a bowl of ambrosia— the food of the gods.

"You like fast cars?" Rich asked, trying to make peace with me.

"Sure," I said. The truth was, I didn't really care about fast cars. I just didn't know how to say that.

"Come on, then. Let's take a ride."

"Uh, yeah, okay," I said nervously. "Be right back, Mom."

"Okay, guys. Be careful."

Rich was in a heavy metal band and had long curly black hair and a goatee. We got in his car and took off, and he searched for a Nine Inch Nails cassette tape as he drove. The name of the album was printed on the spine of the cassette: *The Downward Spiral*. He popped it in, pressed a button amidst the equalizer and radar detector, and turned the volume way up. As the song slowly built to a horror movie type of a melody, the car went faster and faster. The combination of the loud thumping vibrating the black leather seats and the speed on small suburban roads made me feel as though I had no control. I held on to the armrest and door tight, an uneasiness starting to make its way into my stomach.

The song continued.

"I do not want this. I do not want this."

The vocalist now screamed angrily.

"Don't you tell me how I feel! Don't you tell me how I feel! You don't know just how I feel!"

Part of me was scared, and part of me liked the adrenaline running through me, like being on a ride at the Italian festival or on the roller coaster at Palace Amusements in Asbury Park.

When we got back to the party, Rich pulled a few tickets out of his pocket, slapping them back and forth against his hand. "I got you tickets to Marilyn Manson!"

I had never been to a concert, and my mother was reluctant to let me go. She hated that kind of music and anything else she considered "demonic." That included horror movies, Halloween masks, or anything of that nature. My mother was not super religious, but she sent me to Catholic school, and she tried to keep devilish things out of our house, at least in a secular way. Not to mention she wasn't a huge fan of Danielle's boyfriend. But, probably against her better judgment, she allowed me to go.

WE WALKED INTO THE COUNT Basie Center for the Arts in Red Bank, New Jersey, to see Danzig, Marilyn Manson, and Korn. I took it all in: pungent gray clouds visible in the colorful flashing lights; torn black clothes; fishnet stockings on men *and* women; bare chests; clothespins pierced through nipples, eyebrows, noses, lips, and faces; black makeup; combat boots; skulls, satan's star symbols; blood; drugs; loud methodical drums; and beating, screaming, and rage.

The concert ended late, and I slept over at Aunt Danielle's house. When I woke, the bedroom was bright from the morning sun. A white comforter kept me warm as I lay underneath it in my Bugs Bunny T-shirt and underwear from the night before. The door slammed shut, and then the covers rustled on Rich's side of the bed. In a split second, he rolled over on top of me. He wasn't a large man, but his body was giant compared to my ten-year-old frame and felt heavy, *very* heavy, and immovable. He moved his head toward my private area and pulled my green Ninja Turtles underwear down to just above my knees.

My body jerked instinctively as I tried to stop it from happening. I said, "No." That's all I seemed able to say, and even that was difficult. It was as if I were paralyzed, as if I were invisible. Really, I wished at that moment I *were* invisible. I wished I could hide.

He whispered, "It's okay, it's okay," and kept doing what he was doing.

I couldn't talk or move after that. I felt like I was crawling out of my skin. I had never been that scared of anything in my life. I had never felt so helpless. I didn't know much, but I knew I was only attracted to women. Women were pretty to me, and men were not. His beard and mustache had a rough unnatural feeling against my skin, and his breath tasted like a combination of stale cigarettes and morning breath as I tried to lock my mouth shut. I somehow knew that what was happening was changing me forever.

After he satisfied himself, he put his arm around me and draped his leg over my body, moving it back and forth as if some loving acts had just been shared between a couple. "I love you," he said.

I lay there under the weight as my soul began to unravel. I was still unable to move, disgusted not only with him, but with myself for not fighting back. I knew how wrong it was. Every bit of my conscience told me it was against nature, and I felt ashamed. There were no more words exchanged. I was in shock. When Danielle came back from the store, I tried to act as normally as I could, like a hostage unable to explain they are being held hostage.

After that day, I began to learn how to keep secrets and push them deep down into a part of me that no one would be able to see or detect, including myself, if possible. It ate me alive inside, and my life darkened. There were times I wanted to tell my mother, my father, my grandfather, sister, friends, but I couldn't. I held it in and ate to relieve the pain. My relationship with food changed. I learned to binge and gained weight fast. Eating took on another meaning in my life.

"Wow, you got fat!" one little Black girl said when I returned to school that next September.

I'd never hated my body more than at that time in my life. Family members told me I needed to lose weight, which tortured me inside because I couldn't tell them *why* I was binge eating. While I wanted to disappear, I also felt something akin to peace when I ate whole boxes of cereal, half gallons of milk, large bags of chips, huge bags of candy, whole boxes of gummy fruit snacks, and entire packages of Fruit by the Foot. But then I learned to hate the intricacies of my body, and I learned to hate myself. I sat up in the bathtub and grabbed handfuls of fat, disgusted that, as people had reminded me, I was getting bigger.

Over the next two years, my appearance changed. I learned about pain, about depression, and about how to cope with it. I dragged razors across my arms to make satanic stars and other occult symbols while I watched the blood surface above my skin. I relished the pain of the cuts, always trying to feel something other than the guilt of keeping the secret and the shame of what I had done or what had been done to me.

I figured out a way to avoid any moment I might be alone with Rich, and the abuse stopped about a year and a half after it started. I pretended that it never happened, like a bad dream meant to be forgotten. But you never forget something like that. It just lurks there, under the surface, dormant—a ticking time bomb waiting for just the right moment to explode.

I sat alone with Rich years later as a grown man. He smoked crack and snorted crushed-up prescription pills I'd sold him while I counted the money and added it to the wad of cash in my hand.

He asked me, "You want to talk about anything from when you were a kid?" A blackened glass pipe rested in his hand, and the crack smoke drifted from his mouth.

I looked over at him with a cold hustler's stare. "Nah."

He looked away nervously. "Okay, okay. I just . . . Well, the same thing happened to me when I was a kid. A guy down the street from my house. And I know . . . I mean, I just wanted to make sure you were okay."

"I'm straight," I said sternly. I turned around to walk up the stairs, leaving him alone to finish smoking the fifty-dollar piece of rock he'd just bought, knowing he'd need more in a few hours. "I'll be around all weekend. Call me."

The door slammed shut behind me, and I put the money in the front pocket of my Girbaud jeans. I got in my car and tucked the package of work—or drugs—between my legs. I looked in the rearview mirror, getting a glimpse of myself, then lit up a blunt and drove away, gangster rap playing on my stereo and a smirk on my face as I hit the pedal and headed into the night.

FOURTH ROOM

TIME TO SAY GOODBYE

M Y GRANDFATHER TONY SAT ALONE IN THE RE-cliner in the new house my mother had rented in Ocean Township, New Jersey, on Harrison Avenue. The compartment under the fifty-five-gallon fish tank where I kept my boa constrictor, Yohan, whose name came from the Stanley Kubrick movie *A Clockwork Orange*, was filled up with forty-ounce bottles of beer and liquor—Captain Morgan, Smirnoff, Crown Royal, Hennessy, Bacardi, Absolut.

The smoke from the pot rolled in thick cigar papers (either Backwoods, Phillies, White Owls, Dutch Masters, EZ Widers, or Zig-Zags in the white or orange booklet) by my five friends blew out of the exhaust fan in the window of my bedroom. Wu-Tang, Nas, Biggie Smalls, Big L, or maybe even the few songs I'd recorded myself, like "Corrupt" played in the background. We all knew the lyrics to my songs, and my boys recited them along with me to different beats. I'd been asked to perform at high school parties with a microphone and a willing audience, and it felt good. Some kids, like my good friend Tom or a few others, even bumped my tracks in their stereos as they left school in their Mazda 626s or Nissan Maximas.

I snuck into the kitchen that night to get some juice. The blue gel tabs of LSD my boy Jake had gotten us hadn't kicked in yet. As I stared at the back of my grandfather's head, his hair silver underneath his navy blue beret, I felt guilty, sorry to see him sitting there alone. We were always together when I was growing up. Best buddies. He was a second father to me, maybe something even more than that. He'd never had a son, and I think I became whatever he was missing. There was no one I knew of in the world who had as much faith in me as he did, though it didn't seem reasonable considering the direction I was headed.

"You're so talented. Keep creating things, Aj—music, writing, painting, drawing."

"You're special. You're gifted. You can change the world."

"You're so smart. You're so good-looking. You're so strong. You have such a kind heart."

"Stay on the right path, be careful, and watch out. The devil is crafty. It's easy to get lost."

These were just some of the affirmations and warnings I'd hear from him on a daily basis. Those things he said were bittersweet for me. On one hand, they made me feel good when imagining they might be true, but inside, I felt unworthy and uncomfortable hearing those kinds of words directed at someone as worthless as me. They made me feel dirty because I knew my talent was mediocre. The things I created were stupid. I didn't have any gifts, or at least none I could point to. I couldn't even change *my* world, let alone *the* world. My heart was filled with rage, and I was knowingly heading down a path not meant for me—a wide beaten-down road many have traveled only to find destruction when they reach the end.

I watched him sitting there and thought about how I used to take off his shoes when I was a kid. As far back as I can remember, he'd come in and sit down in his chair, and I'd go over to him and untie the laces of his brown leather Rockports. I didn't want him to have to bend down. I did it out of love. I did it out of respect. And I did it on reflex. "Bad circulation," he'd say as I gave his feet a few squeezes, knowing how much they hurt him.

If there was ever anyone in the world I didn't want to disappoint, it was him. He knew I'd be something great, but I wasn't so sure. At almost sixteen years old, I carried the secret pain of childhood sex abuse. I was angry, confused, lonely, and diligently self-destructive. Yet here was this old man who had invested so much of his time and effort into me, who did nothing but give his time when he was running out of it. And then there was me, a kid with nothing but time, yet I took all his time, acting as if I had none to spare.

That realization was too much for me to bear. I put the juice down and walked over to him. My grandfather looked at me and smiled. He had a kind face, and his smile made me think of the picture my mother kept in our dining room from his time in the army. A young handsome Italian American soldier in uniform, he'd gone into the army like so many other young Americans during World War II. I thought of the contrasted picture of him in his art studio, the debonair artist in his thirties at his desk, wearing a turtleneck and holding a pencil from Monmouth Park Racetrack, his choice pencil for sketching. Despite a couple wrinkles, a few heart attacks, diabetes, a bit too much of a fondness for horses, and the resulting divorce with my grandmother Betty, he still had the same kind face with that warm smile.

I didn't say anything. I just bent down and began the ritual we both knew so well. I untied his shoes like I used to—one lace, then the other—loosening them and slipping his shoes off his feet. I placed them beside the chair on the hardwood floor next to the stone fireplace. We didn't have to say anything; we both understood what I was doing and what it meant. I gave him a kiss and a hug and asked if he needed anything.

"Just a cup of water, A."

I went back to the kitchen, fetched him a glass of water, and then headed back to my room to drink and smoke and take acid and laugh and talk nonsense with my friends, as if I had it all figured out. As if time didn't matter. If only I could go back now and do it all over, I would toss all the drugs and alcohol into the toilet and watch them spiral clockwise down into the sewer, where they belonged. I would tell all my friends, most of whom I don't speak to anymore and haven't seen in years, to leave. And I would sit next to my grandfather and talk to him for hours about life, love, war, and Calabria, about pain, hope, and disappointment, history, the news, everything, and nothing. I'd discuss art and ideas, about ways to create, about writers, artists, and musicians. I'd listen to Andrea Bocelli and Luciano Pavarotti carefully, taking notice of the subtle changes in their music the way he did then and the way I do now. And I'd listen even more carefully to his rendition of them, which was partly serious and partly satire, performed in the middle of pharmacies, grocery stores, bookstores, and department stores while people laughed and smiled.

If he were here now, I'd bring him to the café where I'm sitting, writing this chapter, and I'd read him portions of this memoir. We would talk about how to publish it and go over different concepts for cover design. I'd ask him what to do with words, and we would have some pastries, and I'd watch him dunk them into his coffee like he did on those Saturday afternoons at Freedman's Bakery in the Seaview Square Mall off Route 66. He'd go into his wallet to try to pay, but I'd stop him and tell him, "I got it."

I'd show him my phone and all the apps and technology he's never seen. I'd let him use FaceTime and watch his amazement as he conversed with familiar faces he loved. I'd tell him all that's happened over the past twenty plus years he's been gone. We'd talk politics while I drove him around and showed him how much everything has changed and how much everything is still the same.

I'd hang on every word. I'd relish every second. I'd laugh at every joke. I'd appreciate every nuance. I'd thank him for loving me and believing in me in a way I don't think anyone else ever has. But I can't go back there, and he can't come here, and that's how it is in this life. Mostly, we realize things too late.

My mother and I sat in the hospital room with him later that year. We watched in horror as he lay there in a coma with a respirator keeping him alive day after day for months, making a big deal about every subtle movement of a finger, a toe, a lip. His leg had been amputated as another unpleasant consequence of diabetes. I remember the balloons and the flowers, the drives up to Johns Hopkins my mother and I would take to go be with him. I was sixteen then. I enjoyed those drives. I enjoyed talking to my mother. I didn't get to talk to her enough.

I remember the Malaysian restaurant down the street where I'd sit and zone out after smoking a blunt and driving around the hospital parking lot and the surrounding neighborhood, trying to distract myself from watching him die. I remember the coldness of the hospital room and of this life as I watched his life slip away. I remember the stereo playing *"Con te Partirò"*—"Time to Say Goodbye"—in his room while I watched my mother argue with doctors through the glass as tears made my eyes feel as if they would melt out of my face. I remember hurting more than I had ever hurt and living through something I had never lived. I remember my entire world crashing down all around me. I remember losing the last thing keeping me at all stable. I remember the finality of that goodbye. I remember the mercy and the cruelty of the decision I'd encouraged my mother to make as he was sent home on hospice. And I remember the wicked sentimentality of lying with his dead body the morning he died.

I remember.

IT WAS NOT JUST THE death of my grandfather, the drugs, the hustling, or my five friends that kept me busy the summer of 1997. A year earlier, I'd met a girl. I had been with plenty of other girls, but she was my first real love.

I guess I could call it "The Year of Sneaking." I snuck out of my house through my bedroom window in the middle of the night and snuck into my mother's car to drive it around Asbury and Ocean Township. I snuck into school late after getting high and snuck out early to get high again. I snuck into my uncle Arax's light tan Te-Amo cigar box in the dresser in the dining room of our hotel to steal weed. My father and I snuck out of carpet jobs to sneak a joint together. I snuck into liquor cabinets and into medicine chests, and I snuck past parents into the houses of teenage girls. I snuck into places in the hood a sixteen-year-old White boy wasn't typically allowed to go. I snuck past the blue pit bull used as a guard dog to get to Elizabeth Avenue, where I watched crack being cooked on a tiny stove, and I snuck back out with that crack to Ocean Township, where I snuck it into the weed we smoked.

I snuck around with the hurt of the abuse on Christmas and Thanksgiving mornings, when Rich and Danielle would come to open gifts or bring pastries from Frank's Deli. I snuck past my boss, Mike, at Deal Plumbing Supply in Allenhurst, New Jersey, and into the liquor store a few doors down to buy airplane bottles of vodka and get a buzz. Though I didn't really like to drink, I liked to sneak back into work, and I liked hiding the fact that I was drunk. I liked hiding who I really was from myself and everyone else. I liked hiding in general.

But the sneaking I liked the most that year was driving a truck to deliver water heaters before I had a license, past the police on Allenhurst Circle on Deal Lake, and over to Brandi's friend's house, where she hung out most of the time during that summer. Brandi had a beautiful face, innocent big brown eyes, and shorter brownish-blondish hair. She was gorgeous. Brandi was sixteen too, and we were in love. It was the first time I'd felt like that. I'd sneak into the room where Brandi slept, and I'd slip underneath the covers with her and get lost for whole afternoons. Then I'd sneak out to go back to work before she woke up.

Brandi told me she was sexually abused when she was young. I listened to her in detail without ever telling her I was abused too. I managed to sneak past her. I hid it from her, and I hid it for her like I had hidden so many other things. I thought it was necessary to hide how much I hurt inside in order to be a man.

MY BOYS AND I SAT inside a barbershop on Main Street in Long Branch, New Jersey, dressed in our basketball shorts, plain white T-shirts or tank tops, and backwards hats, with Nike sneakers on our feet and big silver crosses, or "Jesus pieces," covered in cubic zirconia meant to look like platinum and diamonds hanging from our necks. After smoking blunts in cars outside, we watched sports on the small TV with antennas in the Italian-owned barbershop.

It was a small room with brown-paneled walls, light green commercial tile floor, and white tin ceilings—a throwback from the early 1900s when a bunch of Calabrian Italians settled in Long Branch, including my grandfather's family. There were two chairs but only one barber, the old man, Frank, who always had a packed house on Saturdays, comprised of a mix of young teenage boys and older men who just wanted a no-frills cut and some small talk. We all basically got the exact same haircut: a fade with a one blade.

We checked our beepers, feeling important, and used the pay phones a few doors down to call God knows who about God knows what. We laughed, and we clowned each other and talked about what parties we'd go to that night and what girls we were gonna get with.

"Yo, that girl Tiffany is into you, bro. Ava told me the other day," Jake said. Jake was a good-looking kid; mostly all the girls wanted him.

"Oh, word? What did she say?" I asked, my face lighting up a little.

"Yeah, I got with her already," Ricky said confidently. "It was aight. Nothin' crazy."

I made a noise sucking my teeth. "Man, when?"

Ricky had a way of exaggerating stories or blatantly inventing them. We all did, I guess.

"It must have been right after that time you snuffed T-Rex for his chain back in the day, son!" John let out a loud laugh. He was a big guy—a star lineman—who let out a high-pitched laugh whenever he thought something was extra funny.

We all busted out laughing. Ricky had told us he'd snuffed—or punched—a dude for his chain back in the day. The kid only had five dollars in his pocket when he robbed him, but the way he said *five dollars*, where he dropped the *F* off the *five* and replaced it with a soft R sound and dropped the *ars* off of the word *dollars*, turned into a joke that is still alive and well in 2023. I can get a good laugh from a few guys if I tell any of them something costs "rye dal."

"Bro, he ain't getting with her! He's basically married already. Brandi lives in his house," Jake said.

Brandi was having trouble at home, and my mother had allowed her to move in with us. She was supposed to be sleeping in a separate room, but of course, I had her sleeping with me.

"Tell her it's a guys' night, homie, and you come with us. Or maybe you could get with both of 'em at the same time." Matt laughed, always trying to be a little more out-rageous than everybody else. He did things like handcuff-ing his hands together and driving a stick shift just in case he ever needed to drive a stick shift in a high-speed chase while he was handcuffed.

IT WAS ONE OF THOSE high school parties where the single mother lets a bunch of kids drink in her house, pretending she's being responsible by keeping a close eye on them, but in reality, she's reliving her youth, flirting with the guys, and getting drunk herself.

Tiffany's voice was really what sent me over the edge. She had this high-pitched ultrafeminine voice she brought down to a whisper that melted me a little bit. I was on the front porch drinking and making out with her when my mother's car rolled up the street with Brandi crying in the passenger seat. I told them to go home and that I'd be home in a few minutes as my friends laughed at my expense.

Brandi was sitting on the couch crying on my mother's shoulder when I walked in the front door. They grilled me about why I was at the party and who Tiffany was. I hated being questioned. I loved Brandi, but I was only sixteen, and we already lived together. My mother chiming in just added an unnecessary layer of complication to an already-difficult situation. I felt suffocated by the duo of mother and teenage wife.

I grabbed a few things and went to head out the door. Brandi sobbed while my mother physically tried to keep me there. She was relentless, and a combination of drugs and alcohol mixed together with the feeling of being caged in by my mother sparked a feeling in me that had been waiting to erupt for a long time.

I grabbed my mother and swung her out of my way. She grabbed me again, and I grabbed her back. I slammed her as hard as I could up against the wall, making a loud thud and holding her there for a few seconds. It was the fear and shock I saw in her eyes that reminded me. That look of horror on her face transported me back in time.

I was in the hallway in the garage apartment on West Park Avenue. It was early enough in the morning that the space was still dim. I was four years old and happy my father had come to our house. I had a Teddy Ruxpin doll in my arms, and there were Saturday morning cartoons on the TV. Bugs Bunny.

I peeked around the corner because of all the yelling, my tiny hand grabbing the counter. My mother was trying to keep my father from leaving. He grabbed her by the hair and slammed her up against the wall hard enough that a picture fell from its place and smashed to the ground. I watched him hold her there by her arms, threatening her and pointing in her face with the hand with the scar on it. Her eyes filled with shock and fear, tears not yet forming but inevitable.

Then my mind snapped back to the present moment, where they were my hands on my mother.

Our eyes locked.

"You're just like your father," she said in a disgusted tone.

No amount of anger management counseling can heal a person of the kind of trauma I had inside me. I let go of her shoulders, walked out, and slammed the door behind me.

That was the year I lost my grandfather, and even though we stayed together for a while after that night, it was the year I lost Brandi, and it was the year I finally lost myself.

It was time to say goodbye to the hugs that warmed like kerosene heaters in the dead winter prison of the Jersey Shore, 1987.

Time to say goodbye to the steam that rose up off the mug in the yellow-and-green retro kitchen of second-generation Calabria in the quiet summer mornings of West End, Long Branch, where old souls taught trivial beauty.

Time to say goodbye to the peanut butter toast that disintegrated into black Sanka oblivion like memories of childhood and smiles about nothing.

Time to say goodbye to riding in the faded blue Honda Civic with wooden beaded chairs, Maxe's hot dogs, Windmill, Strollo's, and Freedman's Bakery.

Goodbye, corduroys.

Rockports.

Tilted navy blue beret.

White five-o'clock shadow.

Digital watch.

Goodbye to the paintings that lay strewn across your bedroom, like the laundry, easels, brushes, finished and unfinished clay statues, diagrams, books, horses, and racing programs.

Goodbye to feeling okay.

To being loved for me.

Ode to Andrea Bocelli

"Con te Partirò."

Goodbye to the laughs.

To the songs.

To the pain.

To the life.

To the death.

Goodbye to the little plastic cups filled with fresh-picked mulberries from the tree in the front yard.

To the sweet and to the sour that stained the walkway leading to the front door that led to your warmth.

Goodbye, sun.
Goodbye, moon.
Stars that riddle the summer sky.
Goodbye, love.
Goodbye, hope.
See you again someday.
Goodbye, mourning.
Goodbye, crying.
Goodbye to goodbye.

FIFTH ROOM

PHARMAKEIA

ELIZABETH AVENUE IS A ONE-WAY STREET RIGHT off Springwood Avenue, otherwise known as Lake Avenue, on the west side of Asbury Park not too far from the train tracks that separate the west part of town from the ocean side. It's more like a large alleyway than a street, comprised of a collection of small dilapidated houses and apartments, pale in color with chipped paint and brick steps falling apart, rusted-out metal handrails, overgrown grass, broken windows, and empty Herr's potato chip bags, forty-ouncers, Steel Reserve cans, and airplane liquor bottles—E&J Brandy and Hennessy—lying around. The occasional syringe, wax paper bags, broken crack pipes, and Chore Boy, Pizza Plus, and Chicken Spot containers littered the street. A little here and a little there.

Something about the imperfections in that part of town seemed more like real life to me, at least back then, than the well-manicured lawns and houses of the suburban town we had moved to, where I went to middle and high school. I think that's because it was before I understood how things really work. The hood seemed openly flawed, from the garbage littering the street to the dealers and addicts hanging around outside. Even the police "jump out boys" understood what went on and let a certain amount happen without interference. It seemed there was an unspoken mutual respect between law enforcement and the hustlers on the corner, at least those who conducted themselves as "gentlemen." Anyway, I was under the naive impression that what you saw was what you got.

The suburbs, just like the people who lived in them, looked nice on the outside, but inside those large homes were the same lonely kids, the same broken relationships, and the same addictions, only their drugs came in little orange bottles prescribed by a doctor and were purchased safely at the local drugstore. In either case, the devil doesn't show up with horns and a pitchfork; he presents himself as an angel of light. The Bible says that all have sinned and fallen short of the glory of God. We're all the same at the end of the day; some people just know how to hide better.

Drug dealers stood outside on Elizabeth Avenue in white tank tops or fresh white tees bought daily at corner store bodegas, like Lee's Market on Ridge Avenue, and baggy designer jeans, like Marithé + François Girbaud or Evisu from boutiques on Main Street like A&J Sneakers. They wore long white gold necklaces that reflected the light from the sun and Air Force 1s or Timberland boots and sat on old beat-up kitchen chairs or green Welsh Farms milk crates as cars pulled up, and money and drugs were exchanged through open windows or fiends (drug addicts) came up on foot. While weight was broken down and sold hand to hand in thousands of small transactions, twelve- and thirteen-year-olds stood on either end of the street as lookouts for tactical narcotics squads or black-and-white police patrol cars. Small five-to-twenty-dollar pieces of crack were chipped off with razor blades and sold from larger pieces of rock in thin cellophane sandwich baggies or prepackaged individually in tiny colorful bags that covered the entire spectrum of the rainbow. They waited to be sold stashed in garbage lying on the ground or in the cracks of backsides.

Jamal stood in front of the small gas stove, a medium flame underneath his glass Pyrex pot, while I emptied a small green sandwich bag of Purple Haze onto the table. Jamal was anything but regular. If he had chosen a legitimate business, he could have easily been a top-tier business owner. No, I *know* he would have, and who knows? Maybe he is.

I broke up the darkish hairy crystal-covered buds as the sticky skunky odor punched me in the face, then unwrapped a Dutch Master, carefully uncoiling the light brown outer leaf. I loved the smell of the cigar paper.

Jamal mixed the cocaine, water, and baking soda as it began to bubble up. The combination of the smoke from the piff (Purple Haze), burning frankincense and myrrh sold at the African store on Main Street, and the smoldering bundles of sage, together with the heavy smell of cocaine on the stove and the Egyptian musk oil on Jamal's mother's skin, all melded into some kind of sweet ghetto potpourri, which ultimately smelled like money. Jamal's mother, Mrs. Jamia, set a glass of "moon water" in front of me on the table. She kept large jars of water in the backyard to soak up the power of the moonlight. Her skin was the same color as Jamal's medium brown complexion, and her hair, styled in grayish dreadlocks, was adorned with vivid red, green, deep black, and brilliant yellow silky material that had a little sheen to it in the mid-August sun. She told me to drink the moon water for protection as she looked at me with a warm smile.

Mrs. Jamia was a pretty lady, even though her teeth were slightly crooked, which added character to her smile, and her voice would rise at times and startle me if she caught me off guard. She was always nice to me and commented on how respectful and mature I was for eighteen. "Why don't y'all dress like this Whiteboy?" she would exclaim. "Y'all can't demand respect from people with ya pants around ya knees!"

Mrs. G burned a bundle of herbs wrapped in kitchen twine—the kind my grandfather Tony used to tie up pork braciole for Sunday sauce—chanting something that sounded like a magic spell while she walked or danced around the house like Armenian priests taking laps around the church with their smoke from the *khoung* (incense) early on Sunday morning before the Badarak.

I drank the moon water while I put the finishing touches on the blunt. I tore the inner paper in half; less paper meant a smoother smoke—another little detail I'd picked up from Jamal, along with so many others. Jamal wore a black tank top with red, black, green, and yellow beads around his neck. He was stocky like me and about the same height—

five feet ten, give or take—with short wavy black hair that he would comb with his hand and a sandwich bag. Something to do with the static.

Their love for their culture reminded me of some things I loved about my own culture, as different as it was. I imagined our ancestors had done business somewhere on the trade routes between Africa and the Middle or Near East. Maybe that's what made us click the way we did.

Jamal had a way of talking that was slow, controlled, poetic, and almost rhythmic at times. He was five years older, and I loved being around him. He was a special person, magnetic, highly intelligent, sophisticated, strategic. From Jamal, I learned to pay close attention to the way I spoke to different types of people. I learned to craft unbreakable chains of ideas and concepts that seemed to set people at ease and keep them quiet while they listened, hanging on my every word. Some people call it fast-talking or the gift of gab, which Jamal always told me I had, but his way of talking was smoother than the nervous stuttering nonsense I heard street guys often reduce themselves to while trying to convince someone to do something they wanted them to do. Jamal had a way of getting a person to just about beg him to do whatever they had initially said no to in the first place.

Jamal's house was small and had a minimalistic kind of feel. I was used to that from my father's one-room efficiency apartment not far away on Sixth Avenue, right up the street from my family's hotel. With wooden floors sanded down and painted and similar-looking walls, everywhere was clean and filled with electric color. There was something about the color, something energetic, something creative. It was as if the entire house were one cohesive piece of art, and the people that came and went were part of that piece. It both contrasted with and accentuated the desperate conditions of the street just outside the front door.

I remember the time Mrs. Jamia gathered some kids from the block outside and let them paint her steps with all different colors of flowers and other designs. Black culture seemed to me to have a special tendency toward creativity—another similarity to my own Armenian culture—and I liked watching those kids laugh and paint. I felt good on those summer days on Elizabeth. It was like a portal to another world, one most White people and I would assume some Black people didn't know anything about. I don't mean the world of Black culture. I had grown up in predominantly Black neighborhoods in Long Branch and Asbury Park. I mean, more specifically, the world of the street, a hustler's mentality, the underworld—call it whatever you want, but whatever it's called, I was totally enamored with it.

We passed the blunt back and forth while we talked. The smoke tasted sweet, with earthy flavors of berry and spice. It was quiet enough for me to hear the birds chirping in the backyard and the muffled sound of Cam'ron's "Come Home with Me" bumping out of speakers on the block. After most things I said, Jamal responded with two words he combined into one smooth-sounding "Oye-ahhh?" I told him about life-altering events, like how Brandi had cheated on me and moved back to Florida and how I was renting this little apartment in Neptune on

Eleventh Avenue and how the crew that lived in front of me was mad I was stealing their customers, all to which he replied placidly, "Oyeahhh?"

I got the feeling Jamal and his mother didn't have many White visitors in their house. I smirked as I exhaled a big cloud of smoke from the Purple. Jamal smiled, showing the slight gap in his two front teeth, a feature that added to the warmth of his personality. A kid named B, who was probably a little closer to my age but still older, with a darker complexion, skinny frame, wavy fade, and a serious demeanor, walked in and put a stack of money on the table. B and I would become inseparable over the next few months. Jamal handed him another big piece of crack with a slight yellowish tinge to it.

"Huh," he said as he tied a knot in the bag with his mouth and handed it off to him. It was a knot that could easily be untied, and I remember thinking how my grandmother had used that exact same knot to tie my tuna fish sandwiches for hot summer days at the pool in the townhome community she lived in not far away in Ocean Township.

"So, you workin'?" Jamal asked me.

"I work with my dad doing renovations," I told him.

"You got construction clothes, like with paint on 'em and stuff?"

"Yeah, we paint all the time."

"I got someone that works at Home Depot. I got an idea, somethin' we could do to make some money. In the meantime, you lookin' to make some more money?"

"Hell yeah," I said, nodding and taking another pull

off the blunt. I eyed the stack of money on the table next to a digital scale and array of different sized and colored baggies.

"Aight, this what we gon do." He handed me a large Ziplock bag and a few hundred dollars. "Ima take you to Boost Mobile and get you a phone. Coke, crack, two different types of bud in there, midgrade Ari"—short for *Arizona*, or we called it Taliban—"and the Haze we just smoked, E pills, those the double-stacked smiley faces—they hot right now—and these little glass vials is wet."

"What's wet?"

"Wet, dip, embalming fluid, leak . . . You know. Quarter water. PCP."

I looked at the large bottle of yellow liquid worth a few thousand dollars on the table. Jamal took a Newport out of its green-striped box and dipped the tip in the liquid. He held the cigarette in the air, and I watched as the white paper from the cigarette absorbed the blond liquid almost up to the filter, making it translucent and a little brown from the tobacco as the cigarette got "wet." He opened the back storm door and rested the cigarette in the sunshine. "Then you let it dry a few minutes. Fifteen dollars a cigarette."

He lit the cigarette after a few minutes, and we smoked it. I could taste the burning chemicals as they entered my lungs. The effects were almost instant. The PCP I smoked that day with Jamal gave me a mild psychedelic experience, a euphoric feeling, along with some kind of boldness. I sold PCP over the years to people who "bugged out," screaming, crying, taking their clothes off, chanting, running, jumping out of windows. I even remember a story about a guy in the neighborhood who threw boiling oil on himself. So many people were never quite the same after that drug. Some, I'm sure, suffer from permanent psychosis, hearing voices telling them to do things—bad things—a type of schizophrenia.

Pharmakeia is where the word *pharmacy* comes from. The Bible uses that Greek word to describe black magic, demonic sorcery. I didn't realize it at the time, but drugs create a gateway into a demonic realm. The book of Enoch, though it's not considered inspired scripture, explains how fallen angels taught human beings charms, enchantments, and the cutting of roots and plants. I think of the farmers in the Middle East, who use a special tool to cut the green bulbs of the poppy, slashing them open so the milky white substance can be scraped and collected in large quantities before being turned into a black gum and processed into opium, heroin, and more recently, the deadliest of all opioids unlike its natural cousins, the lab-created drug fentanyl. I think of the mass murder of thousands and thousands, including teenagers who injected that final shot into their arm and died alone in obscurity.

Jamal sent me out with a phone and a package and told me to spend a week talking to people. Everything in that bag was free. I was supposed to give out samples to whoever I could, along with my new number. When I asked where I'd meet the people, he told me, "Anywhere, everywhere." I was cold-calling people, but in person. I talked to every race, color, and ethnicity, both men and women. I talked to them at the Monmouth Mall, bars, pharmacies, convenience stores, everywhere. Jamal told me to study the people as I talked and listened, and I did. I observed how they moved, their body language, how they spoke, tonal dynamics, language, background. I looked for gaps in conversation to interject questions that would lead to opportunities to give out drugs. It was a one-week opportunity to get a small base of customers, kind of like a launchpad.

I got good at talking to people—really good. At first, I just saw the money and enjoyed the calls coming from my phone, the new clothes, the power of being depended on. I enjoyed the camaraderie, the girls, the high from the life and from the drugs. It wasn't until later that I realized we were selling death. Now when I think of the drugs I sold, I think of pure evil.

I remember walking into small dirty apartments with Jamal, both of us wearing designer jeans and fresh white tees, talking on the newest flip phones, decent watches on our wrists, shiny necklaces, a North Face jacket each. The hood was busy when the government checks and food stamps were traded for dope and coke, on the first of the month. I once watched an old fiend shoot heroin into a vein in his neck because the rest of his veins were collapsed and shot out. One time, I saw a hungry toddler open an empty refrigerator while his mother smoked crack in the next room. Dealers like Jamal, though they were out to make money, also did things that showed the goodness God had put inside of them, like bringing food to hungry kids or giving something out for free here or there.

The truth is, Jamal knew money wasn't real. He always told me money comes and goes. He tore up a stack of hundreds in a little motel one New Year's Eve on Route 66 to prove it to me. I think some of his generosity was an effort to make up for what was so obviously harmful and negative—slowly killing mothers and fathers, brothers and sisters, grandparents and children. We ignored that small voice pointing out the evil and listened instead to music made by rich rappers living in wealthy communities far away from the neighborhoods we were in while glorifying and bragging about the life we were actively living. Now all I can think of are the little kids across the country who will try to wake their mother or father today with their sweet voices, nudging their dead bodies. "Mommy, Daddy, wake up, wake up." But they never will, and those kids will grow up without them and in abusive foster homes in many cases.

Back then, I saw the pain on the faces of Black and White men and women who looked like they were eighty when they were only thirty, when they woke up at three o'clock in the morning to buy another hit in the middle of winter in a T-shirt, looking like the walking dead. There was something robotic about the way their bodies moved, their eyes wide-open, like their souls had been taken over. They no longer possessed a sense of self and were only hopeless shells, looking for the only thing that could bring a moment of peace in a world of pain. I saw marriages ripped apart and wives and mothers become cracked-out addicts or dopeheads. Husbands crying, coming to the hood looking for their wives, or vice versa. Families destroyed. Children displaced.

And yet I folded large wads of cash and stuffed them into my jeans. I put a poster on the ceiling above my bed with money all over it so it would be the first thing I saw when I opened my eyes. We had been selling drugs since we were young kids, and to us, it was all normal. It was just like any other profession, something to pay the bills. It was all I aspired to do. Jamal taught me to sell drugs in varieties, to understand an addict's behavior. We were the type of dealers that would wait outside a rehab center for a dopehead to walk out and give them a free bag and our number. And while the buyers deteriorated into shells of themselves, narcotics were off-limits for us. A dealer who did coke, crack, meth, or heroin was like a pigeon touched by human hands. That meant no more consignment.

Drugs are *pharmakeia*—black magic, sorcery, spells. Drug dealers are deceived into selling death right where they live and count the money while they do it, not because they're bad people necessarily, but because it's normal. Drugs don't only destroy the lives of the addicts, but the dealers too. I thought I was winning a game, but in reality, I was losing. Hustlers think they're lying in wait for the blood of their customers and that it's not their responsibility, but they unwittingly wait for their own blood. They lurk secretly in dark corners for their own lives. No matter how it looks on the surface, in the end, everyone will have to answer for what they did in this life. Money, cars, clothes, jewelry, houses—what does it profit a man if he gains the whole world but loses his own soul?

SIXTH ROOM

Too Legit to Quit

I DON'T EXACTLY KNOW HOW I FOUND MYSELF AT A café in Amsterdam early in the morning with the sun on my face in 2003. It had been two years since I'd started working for Jamal, and I hadn't been out of the tristate since I was a kid, let alone traveled to Europe. It was as if life were driving me around like a city bus, dropping me off at random destinations, some nicer than others.

I relaxed at a patio table, smoking a joint, sipping a macchiato, enjoying the quiet of the morning, and taking in the colorful houses and strange Dutch baroque seventeenth-century architecture of the city. The crispy layered dough of my croissant flaked off onto the white plate and into my coffee as I surveyed a nearby flower shop with clay pots hanging from the ceiling holding rich green ferns that draped halfway to the ground. Greenery on tables and on the sidewalk, with pink, yellow, and purple garden flowers and tulips popping up in the midst of them, decorated the block.

Parked bicycles outnumbered human beings, who walked quietly down the sidewalk, while others on motor scooters and bicycles flew by alongside cars on the clean brown brick streets. I was a long way from broken glass and the littered narcotic-ridden streets of home. The aroma of perfumed marijuana and freshly roasted espresso seeped out of my mouth and nostrils, and my gaze caught on one of the marijuana plants at the flower shop. I thought of my father a few years earlier.

He stood in the upper floor of his warehouse next to my apartment on Eleventh Avenue in Neptune. The room was a large open space with dusty wooden floorboards that were missing in some spots, so you had to walk carefully to avoid falling through them to the bottom floor where he kept all his equipment and tools. The familiar chaos of five-gallon paint cans, an eclectic collection of miscellaneous wooden boards, siding, toolboxes, a hundred fishing poles and lures, rolls of carpet, tackless strip, padding, benches made from scrap pieces of plywood, and two-by-fours stretched across the warehouse. A dark brown pegboard held what looked like a million tools, all marked *MK* for Manuel Kaymakcian.

My father looked serious in a funny way, his face, hair, and clothes covered in speckled white paint from the Section 8 renovations he did all over Neptune and Asbury in tiny one- and two-bedroom cockroach-ridden apartments, where I saw how everybody loved him. A medium-sized marijuana plant we'd grown together from seed stood in a black flowerpot in front of the window. He watered it and delicately touched the leaves and flowers of buds with his thick painted fingers. The sunlight beamed through the large window all around him.

"*Geghetsig eh, cheh?*" he asked. *It's beautiful, no?*

My father's love for growing marijuana resembled the love he had for playing his guitar, for singing, measuring, installing, cutting, building, demolishing, planning, counting, negotiating, saving, spending, buying, selling, writing, smoking, laughing, drinking, loving, kissing, crying, hugging, trying, failing, inventing, persuading, hurting, surviving, living. He was good at all of them—better than I was and with more intensity—and I wished I were more like him.

When he'd finished watering the plant, he asked if I could move it over a few feet. After moving it, I accidentally bumped into it with my foot and watched it fall through one of the holes in the floor. I looked through to where it lay, the plant and roots exposed, the rich dark soil scattered across the paint-stained concrete floor.

"Ajaaaay! Come on, maaaan!" my father said, rushing down the stairs to assess the damage.

That familiar feeling of inadequacy and disappointment, of self-hate and self-doubt, of embarrassment, shame, fear, and failure I'd felt so many times as a kid began to seep in, and just as I was recalling how everything in my life seemed to disintegrate in my hands, the warm feeling of a familiar kiss broke the memory.

Gabriella walked down from the hotel in Amsterdam, gave me a kiss on the cheek, and sat across from me, brushing her long permed gold-brown hair behind her head. She took the joint out of my hand with a playful smirk. Gabriella was a half-Italian, half-Irish girl from North Jersey—a town called Iselin, Exit 131 off the Garden State Parkway. I passed it all the time on late-night trips to and from going to see the Jamaicans in uptown Harlem in New York. That's where all the weight came from: uptown, mostly. All the drugs that were sold in Asbury Park more or less came from New York, more specifically Harlem for us, and sometimes another connect in the Bronx or, if we were desperate, Jersey City.

Harlem had a history of hustling; big names in the drug game came out of there. Brooklyn was known for stickup kids—people who would rob their own connects—but Harlem was a different culture. Our connect used to do something with fashion and would send us back to Jersey with new clothes. I took trips back and forth with Jamal, picking up packages and bringing them back in cars we'd rented or borrowed from customers, who we would pay in cocaine a lot of the time. Whole nights were spent breaking down weight into grams. A pound of pot came in at 448 grams, but if we stretched that, making the grams 0.8s instead of straight 1.0s and fluffing up the bags, it became 560.

We used to get a few girls together who liked to smoke and give them a little weed in exchange for their help bagging everything up. A basic function of mine was to sit somewhere close enough to watch the girls to make sure they weren't stealing from us. I had to make it look like I wasn't watching them when, in fact, that's mostly all I did.

One day, a new girl came walking through the door. She had permed light brown hair, high cheekbones with freckles, and big brown eyes. I stood over at my kitchen counter counting ecstasy pills, and occasionally, I'd look over at Gabriella. She would look down and fidget, so I sat down to talk to her, trying to make her a little more comfortable. Once the formalities were done with—where you from, how old are you, etc.—it wasn't long before we popped a few E pills, and the other girls left. We became inseparable after that night, and over the next month, she got a glimpse into what my life was actually like.

It looked like I was having fun from the outside, but the truth was, I was totally lost in a sea of chaos. I was taking six E pills a day on average, and smoking PCP was a slow burn for me. I felt like I was losing my mind. I'd be gone for days at a time, bagging up drugs in motel rooms, or outside at three or four in the morning selling crack, which I didn't do all the time and was the least favorite of my responsibilities. I'm pretty sure the list of White kids who stood on Elizabeth Avenue chipping off crack or standing outside the Chicken Spot next to the train station selling weed wasn't very long. I stood out in an all-Black neighborhood. A lot of people weren't happy, including TNT, the tactical narcotics team.

I should have gone to jail a million times, but by the grace of God, I didn't. I acted as if I wasn't scared of anything back then, partly because the drugs had warped my perception of reality and partly because I didn't really understand the possible consequences, but sitting here now, I recognize that I was terrified of anyone really seeing me, because underneath the surface, I was a ten-year-old kid drowning and gasping for air. I did a good job hiding who I actually was, but one deep look into my eyes and Gabriella saw me, and it became clear to her that it was only a matter of time until something bad happened.

It was surprising how quickly her family took me into their home. She lived with her mother and father and two younger sisters, and they treated me as if I had always been there. She had a large extended Italian family spread out through North Jersey all the way up to Bayonne, which some people call the best-kept secret in New Jersey. I started working with Gabriella's uncle, who owned a cold cut route. We woke up at 4:00 a.m. and drove to Carlstadt, where we'd load up the truck and then drive with the cold winter air blasting into the open windows and Dunkin' Donuts coffee keeping us awake. We delivered to thirty Pathmark grocery stores all over North Jersey. Seeing hustlers in Paterson and Irvington and bulletproof glass in the bodegas made me glad I'd left Asbury. It was a big change for me. A job like that was a far cry from rolling out of bed at 10:00 a.m. to sell drugs out of my bedroom window in my boxers with a blunt hanging out of my mouth.

Sunday dinners were what I liked most about the life I'd found myself living in the early 2000s. All of Gabriella's family would get together and watch the new episode of *The Sopranos* while her mother or one of her aunts stood at the stove with a wooden spoon, stirring a big silver pot of sauce, meatballs, and sausages—sweet and hot—and antipasto sat ready on the table, along with fresh bread. So much of those Sundays reminded me of my mother and my grandfather, my sister. We used to have Sundays like that too, and it made me feel good, although I always felt like

I was on the outside looking in, wishing it were my family together on Sunday instead. If I'm honest, I still feel like that sometimes.

I was glad to get away from the death threats, the coke, crack, ecstasy, and PCP, the endless nights, and the stress of being a dealer. I liked living a normal life, but I didn't know how. And if it weren't for the incident with the state troopers, I don't think I would have even ended up moving in with Gabriella's family. You know when you're watching a horror movie and the music starts to build, and you know something bad is about to happen? Well, everyone who was around me back then could hear the music.

JAMAL AND I WERE ON our way back from Harlem on a cold rainy autumn day. The leaves on the oak trees passed me by in a blend of magenta, amber, rust, hickory, merlot, honey, and moss green. The color of the trees spoke of hope and change, two things I was in desperate need of. I'd been back and forth on the New Jersey Turnpike many times, but on this particular day, the lights of a state trooper lit in my rearview. I pulled over and took a deep breath to gather my composure.

"Where are you guys coming from?" the trooper asked at my open window.

"Manhattan," I said without hesitation.

"What were you doing in Manhattan?"

"My grandfather owns a jewelry store in the Diamond District."

"How long were you in New York?" the trooper asked, probably trying to catch some hesitation or a hint of nervous energy.

"A few hours. We had lunch together."

"What did you have for lunch?"

"Shish kebab and rice pilaf. Why, you hungry?"

He was a young trooper. I knew it wasn't smart to let him know I was annoyed with his rookie attempt to catch me in a lie, but I couldn't help myself. In the trunk sat a few ounces of coke, 250 double-stacked smiley face ecstasy pills, a vial of angel dust, and a pound of midgrade pot we called Taliban. It was enough to send me and Jamal to federal prison for thirty years. My body shook, and my palms were sweaty. The adrenaline sent shock waves through me when it became clear the trooper was skeptical of my answers, but my heart really sank when he asked to search the car.

Jamal was always adamant about reminding police about proper police procedure. I refused the search and told him I was in a rush and that there was no probable cause for him to search the car. He argued with me for a few minutes, trying to persuade me to give him permission to search the red Cavalier I'd rented from a crackhead. He finally made a call for the K-9 unit, which I knew was possibly a fake call designed to make me nervous enough to confess everything and show him where the drugs were. Frequent TNT stops had made me privy to the game of cops and robbers. In the paraphrased words of John Gotti, "If there was a church robbed, and I had the steeple stickin' out of my back pocket, I wouldn't tell them I did it."

So I sat on the side of the New Jersey Turnpike with Jamal, and as far as I knew, drug sniffing dogs would soon arrive, and I'd be going to prison for a long time. A slight drizzle dampened my face as I looked into the exhaust-scented night. Oak trees swayed in the wind, their thousands of leaves dancing to a rhythm of their own, and in that moment, I felt as if God were there. I closed my eyes and started to pray. Nothing eloquent, just a simple prayer: *God, get me out of this.* A call came through on the radio that seemed urgent, and the trooper told me to "just go." They took off as I slowly merged back onto the turnpike.

That would have—or at least could have been—the end of my life as I knew it. I had been given an opportunity, and I knew it had something to do with that prayer. People on my block knew a lot of weight came through my apartment, and after I got out of that turnpike incident, I started hearing whispers about a few guys cooking up a scheme to rob me. I moved in with Gabriella's family a week later.

AFTER A YEAR WITH GABRIELLA, I had gotten clean—at least from ecstasy and PCP. I was in better shape, and my mind was in a good place. She had received a settlement for an accident she was in before we met: $300,000, which was an exorbitant amount of money for two twenty-year-old kids. We decided to move back to Asbury Park, but since she had come in to so much money, we decided to take a trip to Amsterdam together just for some adventure prior to the move.

Our apartment was on the seventh floor of a building called the Santander. I looked out the window of our bedroom at Deal Lake while I dressed in a black Calvin Klein suit, then walked down to the lobby, over the beautiful mosaic tile, between ornate spiral columns, and past ornamental fountains. I climbed into a new all-white Infiniti G35 coupe. Our building was two blocks from the beach and also two blocks away from my little brother, Raphi, and two cousins, Manny and Petey. Every Sunday like clockwork, I picked them up and took them to St. Stepanos Armenian Apostolic Church in an extremely wealthy town not far from us called Deal.

I walked up the creaky steps covered with thin commercial carpet that led to the kitchen of my father's apartment on Fifth Avenue just down the street from Convention Hall and the BerkeleyCarteret hotel. The apartment was the upstairs section of a house owned by a funny old Armenian lady named Sima Solakian. My father sat in the smoke-filled kitchen, his head down, eyes closed, and mouth open as a cigarette burned his pajama pants. There's something haunting about the memory. I watched from the middle of the staircase as my six-year-old brother, Raphi, took the cigarette out of his hand and put it out in the amber glass ashtray, a remnant of the hotel.

I had started to get my hands on prescription pills at the request of my father and his friends. It was around the same time big pharmaceutical companies were getting rich off drugs like OxyContin and other opioid drugs, when doctors we're going crazy writing prescriptions to people like it was candy. I was twenty-two years old, and I had stopped selling street drugs like crack, cocaine, and ecstasy—at least for the time being. I had borrowed $4,000 from Gabriella and set up a twice-a-week meeting with some dealers on the other side of town. I bought a pound at a time from rich White kids who had a cheap connect to high-grade hydroponics and very strong marijuana grown exclusively in water. I sold it in quarter pounds twice a week, but in addition to that, I started selling prescription pills. Five- or thirty-milligram Percocets or Roxicets; ten-milligram Xanax bars, which could be broken up into four equal parts or sold whole; or five-milligram Vicodins seemed more acceptable somehow. Cleaner. Neat orange bottles with white caps and clearly printed labels from seemingly respectable physicians felt very unlike the powder we bought in sandwich baggies or little wax envelopes with crude labels like *Captain Crunch*, *Blue Magic*, or *Louis Vuitton* from uptown New York City.

The fiends didn't look like the junkies who walked around the streets in dirty clothes with track marks all over their arms. They looked more like my father: a middle-aged Armenian American who worked hard during the day in his construction clothes; who loved classic rock and roll and drinking a six-pack of Budweiser with his buddies, talking football; who had money to pay his rent, at least most of the time; and who owned a few vehicles for work and a fifteen-foot boat he loved to go fishing on. And the dealers looked more like me.

The truth is, gangsters in suits sat around boardrooms and had conference calls about mass marketing a drug to an enormous network of those with the title "doctor" across the country. Those companies had the capital to give out free vacations in tropical islands and other perks while they sold death to America and created the largest drug epidemic the United States has ever seen.

Looking back, I was just a pawn like I had always been, doing the devil's work. I thought I was helping my father out with the aches and pains resulting from the physical work he did and the hard life he lived. I should have known when I saw my six-year-old brother pull the cigarette away from my father's burning pants as he nodded out. I should have gotten a clue when I started using those drugs myself and my relationship with my girlfriend started to deteriorate. But instead, I patted my little brother on the head and told him not to worry, that it was all good, that Daddy would be okay, and then I took him to church. But not before buying the kids breakfast with a knot of money I'd made from selling the same drugs that we're killing my own father.

They say God works in mysterious ways. So do demons.

SEVENTH ROOM

Chasing the Dragon

I HAD LEARNED TO HIDE MY ADDICTION WELL. IT WAS 2009, and my father had gotten me a job at a carpet store shortly after Gabriella and I had moved back to Asbury Park six years earlier. I had been going to that store with my dad since I was a little boy. We knew the owners well, and a steady job had given me a sense of stability—somewhere I could show up every day at 10:00 a.m. and make legitimate money. The carpet warehouse was a large open space, clean with hundreds of rolls of carpet neatly stacked on top of one another on opposite sides of two large adjoining rooms. The carpet rolls ranged widely in color and texture and were wrapped in either thin cellophane or thick plastic wrapping. Bits of carpet fibers, dust, and cuttings littered the smooth concrete floor.

Most of the day, I sat at a cheap desk with a stereo on it, next to a dark blue charging station for the forklift. I rode around on that forklift all the time, picking up the giant rolls with a silver twelve-foot boom and maneuvering them around with surgical precision. Just like anything you do over and over again, it became like second nature, and I did it high as a kite listening to System of a Down or classical piano.

Most of the time, I was alone with my thoughts, listening to music, or reading. My concentration was broken only by the occasional visit from a customer coming to pick up an order. In the desk sat a sandwich bag with cocaine, pot, heroin, and little blue prescription pills marked *M30*, called Roxicets, which I sold to the customers and carpet installers, unbeknownst to the wonderful Jewish family who owned the business and treated me as if I were related to them.

I was high most of the day. I had become skilled at accomplishing my daily tasks and preparing orders for big flooring jobs while sniffing dope or coke in between cutting carpet.

Everything in moderation, I told myself as I opened the small wax paper bag of heroin. I laid the beige powder out in a line on a book I was reading—*Black Dog of Fate* by Peter Balakian, a coming-of-age story about an Armenian American boy who grew up in North Jersey and discovered his family's experiences during the Armenian genocide of 1915. I put down my cigarette and rolled a twenty-dollar bill into a tube with Andrew Jackson's serious eyes staring at me. As I stared back into his, I snorted the line up through my nose, off the part of the book cover that featured a famous photo of a group of starving Armenians being marched to their deaths by Turkish gendarmes armed with bayonets. The pungent odor coupled with the bitter taste hit the back of my throat. I let out a gasp of relief and picked my cigarette back up.

I spent a lot of my free time at the warehouse reading. Aunt Mari had sent me a few books about Armenia when I was fifteen and had sparked my interest not only in reading in general, which until that moment had not been an interest of mine in the least. But also, a curiosity, and appreciation of my culture, history, and language. Reading those books led me to consider my identity, the meaning of life, and various ideas of self-development. Though my actions at the time didn't allow me to reap the benefits of this introspection, the knowledge and wisdom I retained were ultimately life-changing. I love my aunt for that and am forever grateful for the interest she's always taken in me. In addition, I spent hours reading the Bible, surprisingly enough. Though God was an extremely distant figure, I knew He existed at the very least, and I had always been fascinated by the stories.

By this point, I'd mostly recovered from my breakup with Gabriella and had even started a small carpeting business as a side hustle. My father had learned to install carpet from his father and had gone to great lengths teaching me to do the same. From the time I was a little boy, I can remember waking up early at my family's hotel. The hotel cost too much to heat entirely during the cold months, and the smell of the kerosene space heater was a sweet aroma, like the fragrant burning of frankincense and myrrh as far as I was concerned.

"Wake up, *yavrik*." *Wake up, my little one.* "Time to wake up," my father whispered as he gently nudged me to life. My father's beige Ford van rumbled as it warmed up outside.

As the cold breeze whipped off the ocean, I pulled my warm coat and hat tighter around me and down over my brows. The smell of Marlboro Reds and freshly brewed coffee filled the van as my uncles slammed the doors shut. There was a convenience store down the street where we would stop and buy a breakfast of Tastykake powdered sugar donuts and chocolate milk—the ideal breakfast for a five-year-old. My father and his brothers joked and laughed with the Indian store owners and their customers as they grabbed a few buttered rolls and poured more steaming coffee into their cups.

On the way out, my father gave a homeless man with dirty clothes, untied shoes, and a dark dingy beard with patches of white—hinting at the difficult and painful past he'd no doubt lived—a hot coffee and a few dollars, while others shooed him away with their hands in disgust.

"How come other people don't give him money, Babba?" I asked.

"Because they know he'll spend it on booze." He and my uncles laughed.

I watched the homeless man walk right to the liquor store and asked my father, "So, why do we give it, then?"

"He buys food too, *Janik.*" *Janik* is a term of endearment meaning *God is gracious.* "It makes God happy when we're kind, so you give when you can. Everyone has to score sometimes, *haskatsar*?" my father said with a wink and a smile.

I nodded my head and smiled in agreement. My father was everything to me. I wanted to be just as I saw him. I loved everything about my father, and I loved everything about carpet, but mostly, I just wanted to be wherever my dad was. I would have loved whatever work he did.

He was only about five feet nine but muscular and strong as a bull. He could carry giant rolls of carpet on his back up three flights of stairs. My father had his flaws even then, but I couldn't see them, and I wouldn't have wanted to. To me, he was better than Superman, and I liked it that way.

I loved everything about being on the job with him: the smell of burning seam tape; the feel of the carpet fibers on my fingers; the sound of suicide blades being changed in and out of his chrome knife; the thud of his knees hitting the kicker, shaking the whole house: *ch chk boom, ch chk boom, ch chk boom!*

My father and uncles, with their dark hair and tan skin, spoke Armenian that echoed in the emptiness of the new house as they cut large strips of excess carpet off the walls and tucked what remained into the crevice with a hooked knife with a rustic wooden handle called a tucker, finishing the work.

"When can I use the knife, Dad?" I asked over and over again.

"When you get bigger."

"I am big, Dad! I am big! Look at my muscles!"

My father felt them and laughed. "Wow!"

My job, according to my father, was Official Piece Picker Upper—a title I took a lot of pride in. His black toolbox still sits in my garage, and sometimes, if the mood catches me right, I cry when I take it out to use it. Pictures of Dad and me as little boy are taped to the inside of the lid. Sometimes I close my eyes and rub over top of them, remembering those mornings that are now like the memory of a dream.

AFTER I FINISHED UP AT the carpet warehouse, I rushed home to our house on Wickapecko Drive. I was living with my father in Ocean Township back then, and this was one of the twenty or so addresses I've lived over the years. We rented a two-bedroom house with a few additional rooms in the basement. It wasn't anything spectacular, but we made it livable. In the basement was my little brother's room, my room, and a room for Yani—or Yanushka Tanai—a wildly funny Hungarian-born national with a thick accent and long beard and mustache, who was more of an uncle than a family friend and whose stories were the stuff of legends. He had a daughter the same age as my younger brother; they grew up together and later fell in love and got married.

No one really knew about my heroin habit. I didn't show the telltale signs of addiction like most addicts do. I never felt dope sickness, but I knew of it. I'd sold dope to people who'd begged me, and women had offered me sex to get high. As a dealer, I always had dope and never had to feel the symptoms of withdrawal.

Until one day, while I was at the Exxon on the Asbury Circle on Route 66, I noticed a guy who I could have guessed was Armenian. With thick jet-black slick-backed hair and a light olive skin tone, he looked as if he could have been a distant relative, and he had a strange way of speaking that had a hint of familiarity. He was arguing with the store owner over a Western Union transfer. He pulled out a cell phone and made a call.

"*Hallo, hallo, akhberis. Eem dram oonees?*" *Hello, hello, my brother. Do you have my money?* he said in his Eastern Armenian dialect.

I approached him after he got off the phone. I was happy to give him twenty dollars to hold him over until he worked out his transfer so he could buy cigarettes and a drink. It's always a pleasant surprise to meet another Armenian. I glimpsed part of a tattoo underneath his opened-up button-down shirt that read *Armenian Power*, which I knew was a large gang in California. Serj and I exchanged numbers and got together later that week.

Heroin was a drug Serj was very familiar with, though on the West Coast, black tar heroin was more common. We drove around making my rounds, gangster rap playing in his Toyota. He stopped at a Krauser's convenience store and came out with a package of Reynolds tinfoil.

"You ever chase the dragon, bro?" he asked with a smirk as his dark eyes widened.

"Nah, man. What is that?"

"It's how they used to smoke opium back in the day, *dzo*. You know, like opium in hookah."

"What's the difference between that and snorting?" I asked.

"Pshhhh! Completely different, homie. The high is insane. Watch."

Serj took a piece of tinfoil and gave it a slight fold. He emptied a wax paper bag with a *Captain Crunch* logo onto the foil and held a lighter underneath until smoke began to rise, giving off a stream that he inhaled through a straw as the heroin became black and rolled down the shiny foil. Serj breathed in deep and held it. He handed me the foil, and I took my hit. I chased the dragon-shaped stream of white-gray smoke that rose off the foil like some kind of evil spirit with my straw and inhaled it deep into my lungs. I sank back into my seat. It felt like the smoke had directly entered my soul. I exhaled nothing. My eyes rolled back into my head. Shivers ran up and down my body like I was being massaged by hundreds of women's hands at once. I was absolutely in awe of the difference I felt.

After that, my mild manageable addiction became an intense obsession. I smoked heroin all day every day; it consumed every part of me. There was nothing else that mattered anymore. I continued to work and sell drugs to support my habit, but it wasn't enough. It's never enough. Begging for money was the first stop on my expressway to destruction, but I hadn't yet begun to steal—until one day, I got desperate.

Dope sickness at its worst is nothing less than indescribable agony—full stop. Your bones feel like someone set them on fire. Extreme nausea churns your guts. A feeling of hopelessness submerges you in waves of sadness.

I walked into the house, where I could hear my dad playing his guitar. My father had a beautiful beige Gibson Les Paul and would close his eyes and play as if he were in another world, a world that seemed like it was void of all the pain he had experienced in the deaths of his mother and brother, the beatings he'd taken from his dad, and all of the defeats and disappointments he'd endured throughout his life. I swear my father could express what he felt in his heart through those strings. That guitar literally cried for him.

The guitar somehow mirrored the agony I was feeling without words. The amplifier blared as I walked into his bedroom. I screamed, "Dad! Dad!"

He looked at me, making funny faces while he continued to play. Finally, he put down the guitar when I began to beg him for money. Although my father did drugs, at that point, he still had some control over his addiction to prescription pills, which I had long abandoned for heroin.

He tried to reason with me. "Son, look at what you're becoming," he said. "Can't you see?" He walked me in front of his bedroom mirror, where I saw myself—disheveled, unshaven, with long unkempt hair, bloodshot eyes, and pale sick-looking skin. "You're losing yourself, *yavrik*. You don't even sound like you. You're talking like that wannabe gangster you've been hanging around with."

I always had a tendency to talk like the people I was around, almost a chameleon like mechanism. It wasn't voluntary; it was just something I did subconsciously to relate to people. From the minute my father met Serj, he didn't like him. It didn't matter that he was Armenian; my father had a sixth sense for shady characters.

My dad told me he was broke and pointed to the only money he had, which was for the rent. It was in a black wallet with a chain that was usually secured to whatever pants he wore, even though it didn't match the rest of his outfit and looked out of place.

I went downstairs and looked around my room. I started to cry in desperation. Hundreds of pieces of tinfoil with little black marks on them lay all over. Those little squares of tinfoil provided an undeniable picture of what my life had become. Still, I moved on and looked through my little brother's room for money, searching his piggy bank and finding nothing.

I went back upstairs next, to the wallet sitting on my father's dresser. At first, I hesitated. The guilt I felt was intense, but I finally came to the conclusion that it was the only way to escape the pain. I opened the wallet carefully so I wouldn't rattle the chain. I took out a few hundred dollars and slipped the cash into my pocket.

Just as I put the wallet down, my father came walking in. "What the hell are you doing? What's wrong with you?"

A lot, I thought. *There's a lot wrong with me.*

He grabbed me by the throat, and his teeth clenched together. A look of total disgust came over his face as he raised his fist in the air, ready to punch me as if I were someone he didn't know. Jesus said the eyes are like windows into the soul. My dad paused and looked into my eyes just long enough to see the pain within them, and I looked in his eyes long enough to see the pain within him and watched them well up with tears. He grabbed me and hugged me tight, crying as if he were a grieving father with his son's dead body, and that's exactly how I felt inside: dead. We cried together like I was five years old again, and my mind flashed back to an afternoon when I was little.

The people next door to my family's hotel had a son my age. We played with his action figures, ones I had never seen before. I wanted to keep those figures, so I slipped them into my pockets and took them home with me. Later that night, my father noticed me playing with them on the red-orange-and-green shag carpet in the lobby of the hotel, where I was warmed by the roaring fireplace.

"Where did you get those?" he asked.

A shock wave of guilt and adrenaline pulsed through my body. "I, uh, well . . . I borrowed them," I lied, hoping to get away with it.

"You borrowed them, or you stole them?" My father squinted sternly, the way he always did when he was serious about something.

"I stole them, Daddy," I said, though I was terrified of the repercussions of my confession.

"Which hand did you steal them with?"

I started to cry, knowing but not knowing what would come next. "I don't remember."

"Which hand did you steal them with?" he repeated.

"I don't remember which one."

"Which one?" he finally yelled, causing me to hold out my right hand and close my eyes, waiting for the slap.

His thick hand came down hard on my tiny one, making a loud smack. The pain of the slap was nothing compared to the disappointment in his eyes and the feeling of guilt and shame I felt for what I had done. It wasn't often that my father hit me. As a matter of fact, it was pretty rare. But here I was, all these years later, his hand at my throat and the same look of disappointment in his eyes.

And it didn't change anything. What happened after that night plunged me deeper into my addiction than I'd ever imagined possible. A new high and very new low.

EIGHTH ROOM

HEY THERE DELILAH

DELILAH WALKED TOWARD ME AFTER MONTHS without seeing each other. Tears streamed down her face. I'd heard that the guy she'd left me for had overdosed in bed with her earlier that morning. She woke up next to his dead body. We'd always had a chaotic relationship. Some people may have even called it toxic. A lot of that toxicity was probably my fault. She was nineteen when I met her.

I was doing push-ups when she came walking up the driveway to the carpet warehouse. Delilah fell into my arms, crying, out of breath.

"I'm sorry," I whispered softly.

Her strawberry-blond hair nestled against my five-o'clock shadow, and she hugged me tight, the two of us standing in the shade of an oak tree to escape the glaring sun. But the truth was, I wasn't sorry. I was confused. I was hurt. I was lonely. I was angry. I was jealous. I was insecure. I was lost. I was high.

I was a lot of things, but I wasn't sorry.

She had left me for him and broken my heart with no explanation, which seemed to be a recurring theme in all of my relationships, though it might have said more about my flaws than theirs. We had slept together a few times while she was with him, and I made sure he knew about it. I was in an unofficial competition, and now he was dead. The competition was over, and here she was with her head on my shoulder, looking to me for comfort. Helping the girl you're in love with mourn the loss of the guy she left you for after a heroin overdose is not a situation most people find themselves in.

My mother had been living in Las Vegas for the past few years working as a waitress at the Venetian but had somewhat recently returned to New Jersey and rekindled a relationship with Albert, the guy who was around a lot when I was a kid. There was a year left on her lease at an apartment complex a few minutes from the carpet store. My mother hadn't really experienced the fullness of my addiction while she was away and had let me live in the apartment in an attempt to get me on my feet. Delilah didn't have a place to stay, so I brought her home with me that night.

We walked inside, and I threw my keys on the counter. The apartment was clean and decorated thanks to my mother. White walls with perfectly hung pictures, matching throw pillows, and neatly organized furniture gave me a false sense of normalcy and order in my otherwise disordered life. Delilah and I sat on the couch watching TV, neither one of us saying a word. We glanced at each other from the corners of our eyes as if we had just met.

"You okay?" I finally uttered in an attempt to break the unbearable awkward silence.

"I feel like I'm dreaming," she said, her voice breaking. Her eyes filled up with tears, and she stared off into space. "I honestly don't even want to talk about it. Can we just get high?"

She took the words right out of my mouth. I pulled a bundle of dope out of my pocket and set up my tinfoil and straw to smoke. Delilah took the top off a Poland Spring bottle, then crinkled the envelope labeled *Blue Magic* and poured out the heroin, using the cap as a tiny dish and being careful to empty it completely. She drew some water into a syringe and squirted it into the bottle cap. The mixture looked like a tiny puddle of mud with a few bubbles in it.

Our lit cigarettes sat in the ashtray, filling the room with a smoky gray haze. The mundane drone of the news on the TV partly caught my attention. Air France Flight 447 had crashed in the Atlantic Ocean on its way to Brazil, killing all 228 passengers. The news host quickly moved through the details of the crash and then started outlining the dangers of swine flu as Delilah picked up one of the cigarettes and pinched a tiny piece of cotton out of the filter with her teeth. I wasn't fond of needles, but I was completely fascinated by the almost religious ritual, watching while she rolled the cotton into a ball and carefully placed it into the mixture. She stabbed the cotton with the tip of the needle and drew the liquid into the clear tube of the syringe to the line that read *0.2* in bold black numerals. Delilah shot the dope, and her face changed. She sat still on the couch as I watched her fade away.

A warm satisfied smile void of all grief or worry graced her face. "I don't know why you waste it." Her voice was now a feminine whisper, the words slow and methodical, mellow beyond mellow. "I could do it for you." She bit her bottom lip.

I stared into her eyes, and she smiled, enjoying her moment of peace. In that instant, every ounce of strength left my body. Whatever morality or sensibility that had kept me from using a needle finally abandoned me.

Delilah held the syringe in her hand. "We need something to tie you off," she said with determination in her eyes as she looked around the room.

I was wearing a black nylon belt with a black-and-white silhouette of Jesus wearing His crown of thorns and beams of light shining behind Him. Delilah slowly unbuckled it, a seductive smirk on her face as she pulled it through the belt loops of my jeans. Next, she wrapped the belt tight around my bicep. My bluish veins protruded through my smooth tanned skin. I had been subjected to a lot of discussions about religion in school and had been to Catholic and Armenian Apostolic church services throughout my life. The thought of sacrilege was not completely lost on me as Jesus's face stared up at me during that moment.

The needle punctured my vein, and a small dot of blood made an instant appearance in the tube of the syringe. Delilah drew some of my blood, and I watched with anticipation as it swirled together with the brownish liquid. My focus moved to Jesus's face as she plunged it into my vein.

It felt good to give myself over to something, to surrender so completely. No more fighting. No more struggle. In that moment, all of my pain was gone.

It was like I was back in my mother's womb, safe and surrounded with love, before the sex abuse, before my innocence had been stolen, before crime and money, before I'd been abandoned or betrayed, before disappointments and pain, before tragedy and loss. Before life had its way with me.

A tidal wave of warmth circulated throughout my body, coursing through my veins like it were life itself. I had finally found something to relieve me of every pain I had ever felt. I had smoked pot from morning to night since I was a kid, and that didn't do it. I had tripped on LSD and mushrooms and still felt every bit of shame. I had taken ecstasy two pills at a time, three times a day for months and felt worse than I had at the start. I had smoked PCP and felt even more confused about life. I had snorted cocaine and smoked crack, and the anxiety I felt was only heightened. But heroin . . . Heroin seemed to be the solution to the problem. My problem with pain.

Delilah laid my head in her lap and ran her fingers through my hair, putting me to sleep.

OVER THE NEXT YEAR, ADDICTION took over parts of my life I didn't know it could. A heroin addict is addicted to two things: the feeling of the dopamine release that happens when the drug hits the bloodstream, and the ritual of prepping and shooting up. There were times I was so desperate, I shot water just to try to satisfy the addiction to the ritual. I had made a couple of clumsy and useless attempts at rehabs and detoxes throughout New Jersey in order to pacify my mother, but I wasn't ready to quit. Heroin was life. Nothing else could make me feel what heroin did.

Most everyone in my life had written me off. I stole everything that wasn't tied down and some things that were. Friends, family, or perfect strangers—it didn't matter. I was an equal opportunist when it came to money for dope. I sat through all-night interrogations for robbery, credit card fraud, and other alleged felonies. I was collecting half-smoked cigarettes out of public ashtrays and sharing needles with junkies.

Dope sick, miserable, and depressed, Delilah and I sat around for hours thinking up different schemes. Robberies and petty theft were consistent ways to support the habit. The pawnshop was like a second home.

The envelope scam worked best but put me in the most danger. I would call a dealer that I had bought from many times before, enough to gain his trust, and pay him with freshly withdrawn cash in bank envelopes. Eventually, when we got desperate enough, I would hand him an envelope with coupons in it or something else that felt like a stack of bills for anywhere from five hundred to a thousand dollars' worth of heroin.

It got to the point that my mother asked me to go with her to Macy's, and when we got there, she took me to the men's section to pick out my suit and tie for my funeral. Another time, she went as far as taking me to the funeral parlor to choose a casket. "You might as well wear what you like in the casket you want," she said, crying as she walked out of Damiano Funeral Home.

Inadvertently, she had given me an idea for a new scam. After that day, I often told her I owed drug dealers money and that they were going to kill me if I didn't pay them. I technically wasn't lying, and my mother's fear of her son being murdered was little more to me than a vulnerability I could exploit. "They're gonna find me in a trunk or a dumpster somewhere," I would tell her.

And it's a miracle they didn't. But even if they had, there was no one left in my life who wanted me around besides my mother. Everyone else had long since given up on me. She even talked me into going to some kind of religious fundamentalist group in South Jersey. Weirdos who sat around in a circle talking about Jesus. You know, born-agains, Jesus freaks. I remember them showing up at the hotel when I was a kid. I shot three bags before I walked into the tiny chapel for Bible study at Keswick Colony of Mercy, high out of my mind.

To my surprise, I actually enjoyed the conversation. My mother had invited a Jehovah's Witness to the house to give me Bible lessons as a kid, and while I knew a lot of what they said was nonsense, I remembered many of the stories, and as I mentioned earlier, I had spent time reading the Bible at the carpet warehouse. I participated in the conversation in between moments of nodding out. There were about six guys, all clean-cut and well-dressed with bright eyes. I looked out of place with my baggy clothes and unkempt black beard.

My mother's ultimate goal was to get me into the four-month program there. Five hundred dollars for fourth months of intensive "faith-based recovery," whatever that was. I highly doubted that faith in anything would heal what years of therapy, counselors, hospitals, and rehabs couldn't make a dent in. Four months without heroin might as well have been a million-mile canyon someone had asked me to cross.

I was somewhere between conscious and unconscious when I heard a verse that jogged a memory that took me back in time.

"The people walking in darkness have seen a great light; on those living in the land of deep darkness, a light has dawned" (Isaiah 9:2 New International Version).

I was five years old and holding my father's hand. We walked down the creaking wooden steps leading to the basement of my family's hotel. It was midmorning, the hotel empty and quiet. My father and I were the only two people who existed in that moment. Everything and everyone else was irrelevant, at least in my memory.

The basement was cold and had an endless offering of strange rooms that stored all types of obscure items. The dank old concrete and brick was lit only by a single lightbulb hanging down from a wooden beam on the ceiling. A storage area in the very back held a large collection of charcoal that had a distinct burnt smell I could almost taste.

I was absolutely petrified of the basement, and my father was the only thing standing between me and my ultimate fear. He knew what I was afraid of, and I clung to him for dear life. But then he did the unthinkable and broke free from my tiny hand. He ran up the stairs, shut off the lights, and slammed the door behind him. The click of the lock echoed like a prison door slamming shut.

I immediately began to panic. I was too scared to cry. The darkness was overwhelming. The dark was so dark. It was endless nothingness and uncertainty. I couldn't see anything, and everything I thought I knew and trusted I now questioned.

Does my father love me? Does he know how dark it is? How scared I am? Or how hopeless and alone I feel? Will I ever get out? Can I ever get out?

I pounded on the door like my life depended on it, screaming, "Daddy, please! Please! Open the door! Please, Daddy, don't leave me! Let me out! I'm scared! I want to get out! Save me!"

And then the door swung open. My father stood there with his arms open wide, waiting to hold me, his figure darkened by the contrasting glow of the midmorning sun shining behind him in bright beams of light. He held me tight as I tried to catch my breath.

"Shhh, you're okay, *yavrik*. Calm down. Daddy's got you," my father whispered.

"I thought you left me. I thought you forgot me."

"Never, son. I'll never leave you, and I could never forget about you. I left you down there on your own to face what you were most scared of. Fear will paralyze you, Aj, and this life is full of things that will scare you and take your breath away. You have to face them, and you have to do it head-on. You create your own fears. When you find yourself in a dark place, call out to God. He is always with you. Don't ever be afraid."

I opened my eyes just as the Bible study was coming to a close. One of the men put his hand on my shoulder. "Do you want to give your heart to Jesus Christ today and receive forgiveness for all of your sins?"

"Sure," I said, but in my head, I thought that if he knew what I had done and what my life was like, he wouldn't be asking me that.

"Repeat after me," he said, then began to pray. "Lord, I know that you are God, and I know that I am a sinner. You sent your Son to die on the cross for my sins and conquered death through His resurrection. I ask you to forgive me of my sins today and come into my heart and life. In Jesus's name, amen."

I repeated the prayer word for word, just as he'd said it. I peeked through an open eye to watch his facial expression: closed eyes and a smile on his face. Apparently, God knows whether or not we're genuine, and there was nothing particularly magical about that prayer. He told me to come back and that he would be praying for me.

I drove back to my mother's boyfriend's house, where I was now living in Long Branch, and shot a half a bundle of dope. I nodded out with a needle still in my arm. My mother found me, assuming at first glance that I was dead.

Her ideal plan for me was to go into the four-month program at Keswick, but there was a waiting list, and finding me like that forced plan B: another detox in North Jersey.

This last-ditch attempt to free myself from addiction also caused me to finally lose my job at the carpet store. Plus, things were getting worse on the street. I had scammed one too many dealers. Asbury is a small town, and I heard secondhand that they wanted to kill me. I needed to steer clear of the apartment in Ocean Township. So I found myself in another detox with the normal cast of characters, none of us serious about getting clean, just freshening up for a return to the streets.

I left a week later and begged for money outside the hospital to get back to Asbury. I went straight to a house where I knew I could score some dope. After an old fiend sold me the dope, he left, leaving the house empty, the blue commercial carpet stained black and matted down, cockroaches crawling up the gritty walls. The musty odor of unwashed clothes and human filth permeated the air. I hadn't gotten high in a week, and the anticipation was almost too much to take.

I had tried to buy a new syringe when I'd copped the dope but couldn't because nobody had one to sell, so I used a backup I had from someone I knew and cleaned it out with bleach, hoping to kill any hepatitis or HIV that might have infected it. I took a dirty spoon from the kitchen, rinsed it off, and frantically emptied four bags into it. I squirted some water and cooked out the imperfections with a lighter, the heroin bubbling as the vapors flew off the spoon. I drew it up into the syringe, didn't wait for it to cool off, and plunged it into my arm. I instantly fell unconscious, and my head slammed against the bathroom door, making a loud thud.

I didn't just overdose on the magic spell of the opium poppy coursing through my veins like waterfalls of warm water. I overdosed on the tears I had shed as sex abuse stole my childhood, the tears God collected in a bottle. I overdosed on the pain of my family, on the things that shouldn't be talked about. I overdosed on the pint of blood from a hundred fiends. I overdosed on the money. I overdosed on the poverty. I overdosed on the destroyed lives and shattered dreams—theirs and mine. I overdosed on everything this life and the devil had to offer me. I'd had too much of it all.

Don't bring me back. Just let me go. Let this be the last time. Let it be the needle that takes it all away.

At that exact moment, an old man came walking by. Hearing the sound of my head as it smashed against the door, he came inside and dragged me out of the bathroom, then got a pot of water and ice to dump over my head. The frigidity of the ice water shocked me back to consciousness. I took a huge gasp of air and realized where I was.

"Thank you," I said, shaking as he walked out of my vision like some kind of angel.

His Black Southern drawl echoed in the distance: "A'right na. Gon be a'right."

I should have died that day in that crack house, alone in obscurity with no one to help. I should have been a curse to my grieving family and people I'd touched throughout the years. My mother's and father's bodies should have shaken with grief while they stood over a wooden box I'd chosen for myself. It should have held my lifeless body, a thick layer of makeup on my face, my hair combed, my hands folded. I should have grasped a set of rosary beads. Quiet conversations about what a shame it was and all I could have been should have taken place, masked by the sound of the organ at Damiano Funeral Home in Long Branch, New Jersey. People should have knelt down one by one, hands folded. They should have pretended to pray while staring at me, making the sign of the cross they didn't understand out of sheer habit. They should have thought about how their own day would come, and then they should have eaten and drank and carried on with their lives as though I were never there. They should have watched my body being slowly lowered into the ground while someone held my mother's hands as she screamed. They should have ordered a tombstone with some untrue epitaph to make me sound better than I was.

That's what should have happened.

NINTH ROOM

HE CALLS ME REDEEMED

IT WAS 2009. I WAS TWENTY-SIX YEARS OLD. THERE was nothing different about this particular morning. As usual, the second my eyes opened, a wave of hopelessness and misery swept over me, engulfing me like a flood. I lay naked in the bed, the soft white sheets cold against my skin. My mouth was dry, and I could taste the stale cigarette smoke from the night before. Subtle beams of light found their way through the venetian blinds into my dark room, reminding me that my own personal hell had only just started. The open sores across my unshaven face and forehead stung from the salt in the perspiration beading up on my skin. My arms were covered in track marks from all of the injections made over the past few years—death by a thousand cuts.

I lay there in agony, attempting to wrap my mind around the desperation. The physical pain was incredible—my bones on fire, my stomach turning—but that was nothing compared to the dread in my heart knowing what

I'd have to do to stop the hurt. I no longer got high; that had stopped a long time ago. I now shot dope for one reason: to stop the pain of withdrawal. Heroin withdrawal triggers every sort of pain a human being can experience: physical, emotional, psychological, and worst of all, spiritual.

I slowly and reluctantly got up from the bed to look through a small opening in the shades at the quiet neighborhood in Long Branch. The sickness had completely set in now, and it was nonnegotiable. I didn't have a choice.

MY GRANDMOTHER BETTY LIVED NOT too far away in a house close to my childhood home on West Park Avenue in Ocean Township. I had stolen enough change from my mother's boyfriend's coin jar to take a cab to her house. I sat in the back seat, desperate as the cab drove up the long narrow driveway to her little white house. The tiny bits of gravel crunched underneath the tires.

"Wait here. I'll be quick," I said to the driver.

He nodded indifferently, chewing his gum.

She was a classy woman, my mom's mom. Always nicely dressed, with naive sort of eyes that looked as if they hadn't changed since she was a little girl back in Allentown, Pennsylvania. My grandmother had always been good to me. On days I had to stay home sick from school, I got dropped off with her since my mom worked double shifts at the Italian restaurant. She would cover me with blankets and a fluffy white pillow, which always smelled like fresh laundry soap, in a room with a beige leather couch and her paintings on the wall. She'd hand me the remote control to her Zenith TV and give me a bell to ring if I wanted anything. I loved her.

By this point, Alzheimer's had really set in, and although a lot of the time she didn't remember my mother or sister or even know where she was in her own house, for some reason, she always remembered me. She happily welcomed me in, and we talked for a few minutes. In her bedroom sat a jewelry cabinet with some trinkets she'd collected throughout her many years, as well as family heirlooms she had inherited from her parents, whom she spoke of often. Above it hung a picture of her with a big smile posing next to the acropolis in Athens, Greece, a place she had traveled to so many times. I looked at the picture and felt ashamed. Then I opened the cabinet and took a few rings and necklaces and slipped them into my pocket. The sickness was already waning a little just from the thought of copping some dope.

When I turned around to walk out of the room, there she stood crying, her pale face red, her eyes bloodshot, and her eyelids puffy as tears streamed down her cheeks. I was sure she had seen me steal the jewelry. Before I could speak, her mouth opened.

"I want to go home," she said in a dismal voice that cut my heart a hundred times with a double-edged razor.

"You are home, Grandma," I told her. "This is your house."

"No, it's not! I don't like it here, and I don't know why you people make me stay."

I went into her closet and laid out some of her clothes and shoes. "Look, Grandma. This is your bedroom. These are your clothes, your shoes. Look at the pictures. See how many of them you're in?"

She clearly wanted to believe me, but her mind struggled to make the connection. After a few minutes, she calmed down, and I gave her a kiss and a hug. Then I walked out of the bedroom, leaving her sitting on the edge of her bed, maybe even more alone than I was. As I left her there and walked out of her house, I don't know what I felt more, all the pain of robbing my grandmother, or the relief I felt while some of the dope sickness waned as we drove away. I think mostly I felt almost numb to it all, feeling the feeling of not feeling.

After I shot my last few bags of dope, I thought about my childhood and how I had gotten where I was. *How did it come to this?* I wondered. I considered my life and all the twists and turns, the pain of it all, and how pointless it seemed. I was locked in the prison of heroin addiction. It's a serious prison, one with gates and bars and armed guards waiting on top of watchtowers to shoot and kill any prisoner who makes an attempt at freedom. It's an institution you don't just walk out of.

Robbing my grandmother that day, though it wasn't the first time, had somehow made me feel the weight of guilt like I had never felt it before. It allowed me to finally see just how depraved I had become. I was gone. There was no more of me. I was an empty shell, a house of demons, an arid wasteland, walking around in a zombielike state of hopelessness and endless agony. It was clear to me that the only way out would be death. Suicide.

Every morning, it was there, as soon as I opened my

eyes, hanging over me like a giant anvil. The thought that death was the only way of escaping was relentless, and I found myself thinking about it more and more. I was at the absolute lowest I had ever been. Almost every person who had ever loved me had distanced themselves from me. I wasn't allowed in anyone's home because I stole anything from anyone at any time. I had absolutely no strength left as a man. My eyes felt like they would fall out from the tears. It felt as if my soul had slipped into complete darkness. I was lost, broken, hopeless, confused, and overcome with fear, all without even the slightest hope of ever getting out of the situation I had put myself in.

It's funny. I remember people asking me, *Why would you continue to do something that's destroying your life? Why don't you just stop?* There is no other question in the world that suggests a person doesn't understand heroin addiction like *Why don't you just stop?* As I walked toward the train station, images of me jumping onto the tracks and being ripped to pieces flooded my head. I knew someone who had tried to commit suicide that way and survived. The train threw his body twenty feet, ripping his arm off and setting him on a path to a plethora of surgeries. He was forced to live the rest of his life maimed. But the desperation I felt outweighed the fear of that possibility.

The train horn shrieked not far away, eerie and echoing through my body the closer I got. I started to cry as I thought of the aftermath—my little brother over a closed casket, my parents forced to be cordial while they greeted people at the funeral home, both of them wondering what they could have done differently. In between me and the

Long Branch station stood Monmouth Medical Center, where I was born twenty-six years earlier. Some inexplicable force drew me away from the train station and inside the hospital. I walked up to the window of the emergency room as if someone were pushing me.

"How can I help you?" the woman asked.

"I'm having suicidal thoughts," I said, staring through her.

Minutes later, the door was buzzed open. I sat down in the designated chair, and a nurse sat across from me, took my vitals, and asked me questions. "What exactly is making you feel this way?"

"I'm a heroin addict. I don't know. I guess I just can't live like this anymore."

"Have you tried detox or rehab?"

"I've been to detoxes, rehabs, psych wards, and jail. I didn't do any time. Was just locked up a few times. I even went to a Christian rehab called Keswick, but they threw me out. I was shooting dope in their bathroom," I told her.

"Well, don't you worry, sweetie. You're gonna be okay."

Even though my addiction had caused me to have less than my usual interest in women, I could recognize that she was pretty, with her slender figure, long brunette hair, and a nice smile. She looked just a little older than me—the kind of girl I might have married and had a few kids with in another life. That is, of course, if I weren't a broke suicidal drug addict wearing dirty clothes with sores all over my face.

They admitted me into the psychiatric ward of the hospital, a separate wing three floors up. The hospital staff buzzed the door open and showed me to my room. All different kinds of people walked the halls in blue hospital gowns and slippers, most of them heavily medicated by the staff to keep them docile. These people varied in age and came from all walks of life. They suffered from all kinds of mental illness, some of them shaking and convulsing from withdrawal.

My room was empty, with two beds in it. The fluorescent lights had a way of exposing all my imperfections in a way I didn't appreciate and gave off an uncomfortable ambiance that reminded me of jail. The room was cold, and the windows were blocked with some type of film to prevent me from seeing out or others from seeing in. I hated the smell more than anything—a mixture of sanitized hospital sheets with a slightly foul smell, probably the remaining sourness of previous patients, coupled with the hideous odor of hospital food that lived in my nostrils long after it was gone.

The first night, I stayed in my room, with breaks to walk aimlessly through the hallways to stretch my legs and shake a kind of boredom most people will never know. I took advantage of the few cigarette breaks they gave us and avoided conversation with lunatics speaking drug-induced gibberish.

At about four or five in the morning, a doctor came in and took my vitals while being careful to avoid eye contact, looking past me as if I didn't actually exist. He asked me, "Have you been sharing needles?"

"Yeah," I said reluctantly, knowing how dangerous and foolish that was.

"You got hepatitis C from it," he said casually.

The look on his face was one I had seen on so many people. It said, *See, you shouldn't be living this way. This is what happens. This is what you deserve. You're only getting what's coming to you. You should have just quit. Why don't you just stop? I could never find myself in a situation like yours. I'm much too strong.* It was the same look people had given the homeless man outside the convenience store when I was a kid.

Get your life together, the doctor's face said.

He left the room, and I started to cry. I had no idea what hepatitis was. He might as well have told me I had AIDS. I didn't know the difference.

Later that day, a nurse came in as I sat by myself in silence, gnawing on the diagnosis I had received earlier that morning. "You have a phone call, hon." She was a Black woman with a kind face and motioned me with her eyes toward the hallway.

My mother had somehow found out where I was. "Aj!" she said frantically over the line.

"Hi, Mom," I said, sounding like I had been beaten with a stick.

"Are you okay?"

"Not really, Mom." This was usually the point where I'd start with the manipulation, begging her to pick me up and give me some money so I could escape the pain. But I didn't. *What's the use?* I thought. I just wanted to die already. Besides, I was tired. So tired. Too tired to persuade anyone.

"Can I bring you anything?" she asked in the same tone

a mom uses when she asks her five-year-old if she can make him a peanut butter and jelly.

"Um, in my room, there's a Bible on my nightstand. They gave it to me while I was at Keswick. Can you bring me that?"

"Of course, honey."

"Thanks." I went to hang up.

"Aj!"

"Yeah?"

"I love you," she said in a serious tone.

"I love you too, Mom."

IT WAS TWO O'CLOCK IN the morning, and I sat in my room staring at the New King James Bible. The golden letters on the black leather cover reflected bits of light peeking in from the hallway. My room was dimly lit only by the monitors next to the bed. I began to pray.

"God, I know you're there. I've always known you're there, but I feel like you're not. I need to know, really know, that you're real and that you can hear me. I need you to say something."

I opened the Bible, and in my mind, I was both daring and hoping that God would actually say something that related to my life. I opened it up to a random page in the middle. The thin, almost transparent paper made a distinct crinkling sound as the pages turned that was somehow sweet to me. The page was blanketed with bold black print broken up by verse numbers.

Psalm 88
A Prayer for Help in Despondency

O Lord, God of my salvation,
I have cried out day and night before You.
Let my prayer come before You;
incline Your ear to my cry.
For my soul is full of troubles,
and my life draws near to the grave.
I am counted with those who go down to the pit;
I am like a man who has no strength,
adrift among the dead,
like the slain who lie in the grave,
whom You remember no more,
and who are cut off from Your hand.
You have laid me in the lowest pit,
in darkness, in the depths.
Your wrath lies heavy upon me,
and You have afflicted me with all Your waves. Selah.
You have put away my acquaintances far from me;
you have made me an abomination to them.
I am shut up, and I cannot get out;
my eye wastes away because of affliction.
Lord, I have called daily upon You;
I have stretched out my hands to You.
Will You work wonders for the dead?
Shall the dead arise and praise You? Selah.
Shall Your loving kindness be declared in the grave?
Or Your faithfulness in the place of destruction?

Shall Your wonders be known in the dark?
And Your righteousness in the land of forgetfulness?
But to You I have cried out, O Lord,
and in the morning my prayer comes before You.
Lord, why do You cast off my soul?
Why do You hide Your face from me?
I have been afflicted and ready to die from my youth;
I suffer Your terrors;
I am distraught.
Your fierce wrath has gone over me;
Your terrors have cut me off.
They came around me all day long like water;
They engulfed me altogether.
Loved one and friend You have put far from me,
And my acquaintances into darkness.

As I read those words, the outer stone layer surrounding my heart cracked and crumbled into a million pieces as if shattered by a divine hammer. If I would have written God a letter to explain what I was feeling, I couldn't have articulated it better than that. My eyes wasting away from grief; shut in, not able to get out; acquaintances being separated from me; terrors engulfing me like a flood; darkness as my closest friend. I was finally broken, and in that brokenness, I acknowledged, with humility, the grave place my choices had put me in. God opposes the proud but gives grace to the humble. It was as if I were locked in that basement all over again. Only it wasn't the harmless darkness of a basement. The Bible describes hell as "outer darkness," and I was almost there. Although I had been suicidal, the truth was that I was scared to die.

Something snapped within me, and I began to cry like a child, unable to breathe as I let out all the years of pain and confusion. I unleashed it all upon God, thrusting it all before His feet.

My knees and face on the cold hospital floor, tears and saliva dripping onto the tiles, I began to pray. "I believe, Lord! I can't do this anymore!" My voice shook. "I'm sorry, Lord! I'm so sorry! Save me! Please save me!" I cried out as if I were drowning.

And at that very moment, I felt a physical hug just as I had when my father opened that basement door all those years ago. Jesus held me in His arms in that room, and it was like He had always been waiting there. Though I was a grown man, I'd found myself to be a lost little boy, pounding on the door, my life hanging in the balance, crying out for mercy, begging to be rescued, and my heavenly Father opened the door and picked me up.

I wasn't scared to die anymore; I was no longer held hostage by the fear of death we all face. I was free. I had been called so many things throughout my life. I had been called fat, a loser, weirdo, degenerate, criminal, a waste of life, scumbag, and a drug addict. Satan himself called me guilty, and I had even called myself a number of those things. But it didn't matter anymore what anyone called me, because Jesus? Well . . . He calls me redeemed.

❧

WHEN I WOKE UP THE next morning, the person responsible for taking insurance information told me I was being discharged. I begged her to let me stay a few extra days, and in reply, she gave me a list of phone numbers for local detoxes and rehabs and told me I could use their phone. There were ten on the list, and I called every one of them.

"No available beds," I heard at the end of each call.

I wanted to do the right thing. I wanted to go to rehab. I wanted to get clean because I didn't realize I already was clean. I had been washed in the blood of Jesus, and you can't get any cleaner than that.

There was one more option, but I couldn't bring myself to even consider it a possibility. I had gone to that Christian rehab in South Jersey eight months prior, but I'd snuck in a bundle of dope and had been caught shooting up in their bathroom and was asked to leave.

Out of options and feeling defeated, I walked through the hallway with the few items I had in a small mesh bag. I steeled my face, determined to go back and hit the street. "Buzz me outta here!" I said obnoxiously when I reached the door to the ward.

The nurse moved her hand toward the buzzer that would let me back out onto the street. When she was mid-reach, the phone rang, redirecting her attention. She picked it up. "Hello? Arman? Yes. Yes, as a matter of fact, he's right in front of me." She smirked. "It's for you."

I lifted a brow in question as I put the phone to my ear. "Hello?"

"Arman! It's Jim Freed. How are we doing?" Jim was the director of admittance at Keswick Colony of Mercy.

"Not so good, Chaplain . . ." I told him what was going on.

"Well, it's a funny thing, Arman. The list to get in here is a mile long, but something strange happened to me last night."

"What happened?"

"God woke me up out of a dead sleep and told me He wants you to come back to this place."

I felt like I was in the twilight zone! I had prayed for God to save me in the middle of the night, and He had moved heaven and earth to do it.

TENTH ROOM

BROKEN CHAINS

I SAT IN MY MOTHER'S SILVER HONDA ACCORD IN what felt like my grave clothes: an old pair of jeans, a black T-shirt, and an old military jacket my mother's boyfriend let me have that had belonged to his father. The ride to Keswick was only forty-five minutes south from Long Branch but felt like an eternity. It was only my third day clean. I had died and been resurrected, and I didn't yet understand. My heart sat in my throat, and my stomach was in a flu-like state. The anxiousness that came with the thought of arriving at a four-month rehab was beyond my full comprehension. It's not that I hadn't been to a rehab before; I had been to many, but never with the intention of staying for the entirety of the program and actually changing my life. This felt different. It felt *real*.

Outside the window, the cloudy blue sky stretched like a canvas knifed through by row after row of passing oak trees, which lined either side of the Garden State Parkway. The white traffic lines flew past me one by one, and the unreasonable but still very real thought of opening the door and jumping out dominated my imagination.

We pulled into the driveway, passing the small white chapel, where I'd attended the original Bible studies that had set this all in motion, and a rugged wooden cross standing firmly next to a sign that read *Colony of Mercy,* *"In this place I will give thee peace."*

Peace. I didn't know the meaning of the word. Maybe I never had.

Keswick is set in the middle of a pine forest in southern New Jersey. It was founded in 1897 by a Christian man named William Raws. It was his vision to create a place where men might find peace through faith in Jesus and become a new creation. It is the oldest residential addiction recovery program in the United States.

I was greeted at the door by Chaplain Jim Freed. A man named Charles stood by his side. Chaplain Freed was an alcoholic back in the day and had been saved many years ago. He had a white mustache and beard, a welcoming smile, and an authentic feel about him. Charles, an older Black man, was on an extended stay at Keswick called the Discipleship Program. Charles was in his late sixties and had been addicted to crack and cocaine most of his life. His teeth, or lack thereof, bore the evidence of his years-long struggle with addiction. Charles had been in charge of searching my bags during my last stay at Keswick and didn't seem very thrilled to see me return.

"Okay, Mom. Thanks," I said somberly as I gave her a hug goodbye.

She squeezed me tight and gave me a kiss on the cheek, followed by a touch on my face. She sucked in her cheeks and pursed her lips. She'd been making that face since I was a little boy. It was a facial expression that meant *I love you so much I can't stand it.* I had put my mother through a lot: stealing from her, manipulating her, taking her car, bullying her into giving me money, screaming, yelling. My addiction had also put a major strain on her relationship with Albert. She hadn't always done things perfectly as a mother, but she wore herself out working double shifts when I was growing up, trying her best as a single mom to give us a decent life. What she did was commendable. She'd done the best with whatever she knew and had been a big part of getting me to where I was. She'd paid for lawyers, medications, debts, and a lot more, and for that, I am grateful.

"The colony" referred to the living quarters for the forty men in the program. The building had an intense quietness about it, partly because it was the middle of the day and all the men were working and partly because it was void of any televisions or other distractions. Chaplain Freed walked with me through the small building, showing me the various rooms.

"So, Arman, we gotta figure out what kind of a job we should give you," he said with a bright smile, then began to rattle off some of the positions.

I stopped him. "My family owned a restaurant when I was a kid, and I'm pretty good in the kitchen." I waited expectantly for my desired position to be sealed.

"Kitchen, huh? Hmm . . . You're gonna be cleaning the

bathrooms, Arman. Yeah, that's just the job for you! Come on." He nudged me forward and continued the tour.

Later that night, I met the rest of the guys. In the fireplace room, everyone sat around on the two couches and a few chairs and told war stories from their time in the street. The earthy tones of the room and crackling fire created a cozy atmosphere. The occasional clunk resounded when a log fell to the soot-covered hearth.

I listened to the conversations of men who had already completed weeks or months of recovery. I answered some questions when they asked me and dropped an f-bomb.

"Whoa, whoa," they said. "Bro, you gotta watch that around here."

"Watch what?" I said with a sneer.

"Cursing, bro. We don't curse here."

I sucked my teeth. "If I can't curse, I can't talk."

I walked to my room, annoyed by their rebuke. I shared a room with a big Puerto Rican guy named Santiago who taught me to make my bed as soon as I woke up and vacuum the tiny room on the days it was my turn.

"Come on, yo. Get up. Time to wash your mouth," he said the next morning.

At first, I didn't know what he was talking about, but I found out that *washing your mouth* meant brushing your teeth.

THE FIRST FEW WEEKS FELT like pure hell on earth. Everything happened in slow motion, and my body was in constant agony. Physically speaking, heroin withdrawal is similar to very extreme flu symptoms. It's worse than that, but that's the best way I can describe it. And that's the easy part.

I didn't sleep for at least the first two weeks. I lay awake all night, tossing and turning, unable to get comfortable. Sleep deprivation can have hallucinogenic effects, and your mind will play tricks on you. At first, I tried to remedy the torture by sneaking out of my room. I would go outside and collect a few pieces of firewood, then throw them onto the remaining embers and watch the flames dance as I tried to sleep on all four couches. Still unable to sleep and tormented by the insomnia, I'd head to the bathroom and enter one of the showers, then lie on the floor. I'd block the drain with my body to fill up the shallow tub, letting the hot water hit me for an hour or more. The lack of sleep wreaked havoc on my already dope sick mind and body.

My job was to clean up around the colony: emptying garbage cans, vacuuming, sweeping floors, cleaning windows. I hadn't cleaned my own bathroom in years, let alone one shared by forty guys. One day about a week and a half into my stay, I was cleaning a filthy toilet in one of the bathroom stalls. Chills ran through my body, and a cold sweat dripped off me as the smell of feces and industrial cleaning detergent made me gag while I scrubbed. I sat on the toilet, exhausted, frustrated, and overwhelmed, then started to cry.

The prayer was quick and not at all eloquent: "I can't do this, God. I don't have the strength or willpower."

The thought of transforming my life at that moment was an absolute impossibility. I walked out of the bathroom determined to quit. Then I looked up and saw a framed picture that read: *He gives power to the weak, and to those who have no might He increases strength. Even the youths shall faint and be weary, and the young men shall utterly fall, but those who wait on the LORD shall renew their strength; they shall mount up with wings like eagles; they shall run and not be weary; they shall walk and not faint, Isaiah 40:29-31.*

This was one of the very first times I could sense God was speaking to me directly. For years I had heard people claim God "spoke to them," and it sounded ridiculous. What did they mean? I would think to myself, *Do they hear voices? Are they insane?* But now I knew and was sure in my heart that God was telling me to be patient and not to leave. He was promising to give me strength if I waited on Him.

I was horrible at cleaning—I can admit that—and guys began to complain about empty toilet paper rolls and the general disorder of the bathroom. One day, in walked my counselor, Chaplain Roman, in his beautiful black suit and Dolce & Gabbana eyeglasses. Chaplain Roman had been a Puerto Rican stickup kid from Brooklyn before he was saved, and he'd spent much of his youth robbing people at gunpoint for dope money and committing other crimes. This was a guy whose life had been completely transformed. He was an intense person; he knew what he'd been saved from and what he'd been forgiven for. He was stern and serious about Jesus. I would go as far as calling him a soldier. He would call a man out to his face in a heartbeat.

"Yo, what's the problem? I'm getting all these complaints, especially about the toilets. What's goin' on?"

"I don't know. I cleaned them," I said.

"Come on. Show me." He motioned me toward the stall. I took the toilet brush and lightly brushed the inside of the bowl, being extremely careful not to get any toilet water anywhere near me.

Chaplain Roman took off his suit jacket and hung it on the silver hook in the bathroom stall. Then he unbuttoned the sleeves of his shirt and rolled them up. For a minute, I was reminded of how Rich used to undress himself abruptly without any warning before the abuse would start.

Chaplain Roman got on his knees and began to scrub the inside and outside of the toilet bowl, reaching behind and underneath, scrubbing with his face almost in the toilet. Then he got up, fixed his sleeves, and put his jacket back on. "I want you to clean these toilets as if Jesus Himself were going to use them." Then he patted me on the shoulder and walked out.

It was real humility—not the fake kind where people insult themselves in a fallacious sort of way in order to garner praise, but real, genuine humility. He had an attitude and a heart willing to work for something larger than himself—much larger, like the creator of the universe. Many people act as if the universe *is* God or that they themselves are what the universe revolves around rather than worshiping the one who created it and giving honor to the one who sits above it and holds it all together.

I had been solely focused on myself for so long. I completely disregarded everyone else and how my actions made them feel in order to get what I needed. I had lost the ability to see God and to see other people and care about their needs above my own. I realized in that moment that the world didn't revolve around me and that the way to the top in God's economy was through the bottom.

"God opposes the proud but shows favor to the humble. Humble yourselves, therefore, under God's mighty hand, that He may lift you up in due time" (1 Peter 5:5-6 NIV).

OVER THE NEXT FEW NIGHTS, the insomnia continued. I tossed and turned on my mattress night after night, the sheets damp from the sweat that poured out of my body. Restless and desperate, I wanted and needed rest but was totally unable to attain it. I fell asleep occasionally for a few minutes at a time, and when I did, I was tormented with night terrors. It was like being harassed by demons, a sensation that melded together with the time I spent awake.

I decided since I couldn't sleep, I was going to open my Bible and start reading. So there I sat in the fireplace room, lit by the glow of the flames and the warmth of Jesus, night after night, reading whole books of the Bible, completely mesmerized, turning page after page, unable to put it down. My roommate, partly out of mercy and partly because he was tired of me disturbing his sleep, showed me a verse in his red-letter Bible, which specifically notated in bloodred font all of Jesus's actual words.

"Come to me, all you who are weary and burdened, and I will give you rest. Take my yoke upon you and learn from me, for I am gentle and humble in heart, and you will find rest for your souls. For my yoke is easy and my burden is light" (Matthew 11:28-30 NIV).

I prayed and asked God for rest in Jesus's name—not only physical rest, but rest from the years of chaos that addiction brings, rest from the losses, the disappointments, the lying, the stealing, the abuse, the ungodly relationships, the betrayal, all of the pain and the heartache. I prayed He would help me understand everything I was reading. And then I began sleeping through the night. My body felt better. My mind no longer felt as chaotic as it always did. I started to write letters to my little brother, Raphi, and to the rest of my family. I began to understand the true meaning of the word *peace*. Peace with God was peace inside myself. That's really what I wanted all those times I shot dope: peace.

Even if I didn't fully understand it yet, I was being transformed by the renewing of my mind. As I read, I learned more and more, and as I learned, I grew in faith. I prayed together with the other men and saw families that had been destroyed by drugs and alcohol reunited, husbands kissing wives who'd previously wanted nothing to do with them and fathers playing with kids they had abandoned. I watched their kids' angelic faces light up with huge smiles as they pointed to a father who had been absent, saying, "That's my daddy," and gleaming with pride. I was reminded of a verse from the book of Proverbs that says, "Children's children are the crown of old men; and the glory of children are their fathers" (Proverbs 17:6 King James Version).

Prior to me being saved, there had been nothing particularly funny about my life, but during those months at Keswick, I found myself laughing out loud for the first time in a long time and enjoying things like the sunset as if I had never seen one before. I became more than friends with the guys in the colony. We were all part of God's family. We were brothers. We prayed together, sang together, worshiped together, ate together, and laughed and cried together. It wasn't just an improvement on my old self; it was a complete death and resurrection to new life in Jesus Christ.

PART OF THAT NEW LIFE involved regular counseling sessions, and I was forced to remember a lot of things I would just as soon forget. My time at Keswick was coming to an end, but before it did, God had a major item He wanted to iron out. I walked into Chaplain Roman's office one day for a session, and something miraculous happened. I sat in the chair and gave him general answers, enjoying the conversation, when all of a sudden, he asked, "Were you ever sexually abused as a child?"

I had never told anyone about what had happened to me as kid. I was afraid people would think I was gay. But here it was—my opportunity to let it out.

"Yeah, I was," I said.

"You ever invite a girl over to your apartment?"

"Yes," I answered, confused.

"Me too. You know, sometimes my apartment would be a mess, and I'd throw everything in the closet and slam the door shut, and you know, no harm, right? She'd come over and say, 'Man, this looks great. Nice place,' but inside, that closet was just a mess! You know?"

I nodded. "Yeah."

"Arman, Jesus walks right past the clean apartment and points to the closet. He opens it up and says, 'You got some stuff! Some junk! Some mess that needs to come out!' You get that?"

I nodded again.

Then he dropped seven words that came down like a sledgehammer. "What exactly did he do to you?"

A lump formed in the back of my throat as I thought of the details. At first, I couldn't speak. I just cried with my hands covering my face, ashamed and humiliated. But then, as I began to confess the details, it felt like a million pounds were being lifted off my shoulders.

"Arman, what he did to you was pure evil, hideous. A horrible, horrible thing that should never happen to a child. Are you able to forgive him for what he's done?"

Forgiveness! I thought. "He doesn't deserve forgiveness!"

"I know he doesn't, but neither did I, and neither did you. We are sinners, Arman, saved by grace through faith in Jesus Christ." Chaplain Roman opened his Bible and began to read a parable from the book of Matthew.

Matthew 18
Parable of the Unforgiving Debtor

Then Peter came to him and asked, "Lord, how often should I forgive someone who sins against me? Seven times?"

"No, not seven times," Jesus replied, "but seventy times seven!

"Therefore, the Kingdom of Heaven can be compared to a king who decided to bring his accounts up to date with servants who had borrowed money from him. In the process, one of his debtors was brought in who owed him millions of dollars. He couldn't pay, so his master ordered that he be sold—along with his wife, his children, and everything he owned—to pay the debt.

"But the man fell down before his master and begged him, 'Please, be patient with me, and I will pay it all.' Then his master was filled with pity for him, and he released him and forgave his debt.

"But when the man left the king, he went to a fellow servant who owed him a few thousand dollars. He grabbed him by the throat and demanded instant payment.

"His fellow servant fell down before him and begged for a little more time. 'Be patient with me, and I will pay it,' he pleaded. But his creditor wouldn't wait. He had the man arrested and put in prison until the debt could be paid in full.

"When some of the other servants saw this, they were very upset. They went to the king and told him everything that had happened. Then the king called in the man he had forgiven and said, 'You evil servant! I forgave you that tremendous debt because you pleaded with me. Shouldn't you have mercy on your fellow servant, just as I had mercy on you?' Then the angry king sent the man to prison to be tortured until he had paid his entire debt.

"That's what my heavenly Father will do to you if you refuse to forgive your brothers and sisters from your heart" (Matthew 18:21-35 New Living Translation).

"You have been forgiven for so much debt, Arman, so much that you have done in your life," Chaplain Roman said when he'd finished. "It is only right that you forgive those who've sinned against you, and in that forgiveness, you will find freedom from what has weighed you down all these years. I want you to write a letter to the man who did this to you. You're not going to send it to him; you're just going to speak your mind, pray, and find it in your heart to forgive him. Then you can burn it."

I wrote the letter in the fireplace room late that night. Then I threw the letter into the flames, watching the carefully crafted blue cursive letters, the representation of years of internal pain that had poured out of me like a flood, disappear into smoke and white ash and carry themselves up the chimney. I felt like a demon had left my body. I had been harboring this negative emotion from the time I was ten years old, and now it was gone, just like that. When I decided to forgive, it was as if I were given the key to a master lock. I simply turned the key and opened a new chapter in my life.

FOUR MONTHS HAD GONE BY. Initially, all I'd wanted to do was stop using heroin. What I got was so much more. Jesus had given me new life. The pain was gone. I had been set free. God had touched every part of my life. After completing the program, Keswick held a graduation ceremony, where they presented me with a beautiful black leather-bound New King James Bible as a token of the achievement I had made by God's grace. There was only one person in the world I could think of giving it to. I gave it to my mother.

I stood in front of the mirror in my room while my family waited in the chapel for the ceremony to begin. I put my suit jacket on, straightened my tie, and crafted the knot carefully, making sure the dimple was perfect. My hair was nicely trimmed, my face as smooth as a newborn baby's, my skin a clear healthy olive tan. I looked around my tiny room, thinking about all that had happened, thanking God for what He had done. I shut the door, giving glory to God for saving me and feeling proud of myself for the biggest accomplishment I had made in my life. I had shed blood, sweat, and tears throughout those four months. I'd quit heroin cold turkey, with no drugs to wean me off or even a television to distract me. I had nothing but God's grace and the grit and determination to be obedient to Him. I had finished something, saw it through to the end, tasted real victory for the first time maybe ever. I was ready to go home and start my new life. God had accomplished in four months what teams of physicians and experts couldn't have accomplished in a lifetime.

I walked down the dirt road toward the ceremony in the tiny chapel where I'd once nodded out after shooting heroin with a Jesus belt wrapped around my arm, excited to see what would happen next. As the doors to the chapel opened, the light hit my face, and I walked through yet another door that God had opened for me.

ELEVENTH ROOM

NO SLEEP TILL BROOKLYN

I LAY THERE FLOATING IN THE IMMENSE AND LIMIT-less Atlantic Ocean, gazing up at the sky, a gorgeous blue frontier with accents of various colors and white clouds draped across it. The cold ocean water on my skin was a relief from the heat of the sun. My body moved calmly with the waves in a serene sort of dance, and the taste of sweet mangos I'd bought at the 7-Eleven on Main Street still lingered fresh in my mouth. The waves crashed onto the shore as my father stood on the jetty, fishing for fluke while my brother walked the well-known route up and down the rocky crevices we'd grown up on.

It was as if I had never experienced any of it before. Re-turning home after so many months was an exciting time in my life. I didn't even drop off my suitcase after Keswick. Instead, I went straight to Eighth Avenue Asbury Park. My father, my little brother, and I were the only souls on the entire beach. I hadn't seen the ocean in four months. My mind was clear, my vision was sharp, and all of my senses were heightened. If there's one thing heroin does, it makes you numb. I hadn't felt anything in so long. In a word, I just felt gratitude. I was thankful to be alive, thankful to be free from drugs, thankful to be on the beach. Just thankful. I knew I should be dead or in jail, and every minute I lived and breathed felt like it was borrowed.

Now came the challenge: all of the old people and places, all of the old things.

I had decided to stay with my father at first. He was living in a new place on Willow Avenue in Long Branch. Though my mother's house would've been more comfortable, she tended to be a bit overbearing and naggy. I thought it might be a little much upon my arrival home.

I chose to sleep on the floor of my father's tiny apartment. It was a big change from Keswick. The stale cigarette smell was almost unbearable to me now after not smoking for months. I slept on an old Persian rug my grandfather had given my dad, its symbols and layered borders made up of rich vegetable-dyed colors that told a story, as if the rug were a teacher of the people who had woven it by hand. The first night, the bedbugs attacked me so viciously I couldn't sleep. My body became covered in rows of itchy welts that drove me onto the front porch. I had read about the Armenians' struggle through the deserts on death marches toward Deir ez-Zor, Syria, bedbugs tormenting whatever rest they managed to get when not moving from place to place under the unbearable heat of the desert sun. There was a roll of gray duct tape on the coffee table that my father would use to catch a few at a time crawling up the walls. My little brother slept on a mattress in his small bedroom, placed a foot away from the wall as an attempted barrier between him and the tiny tormentors.

Though my father and my stepmother, Karen, usually lived in the middle of bad neighborhoods, they always kept everything clean and tidy, reminiscent of the meticulous nature of my father's mother. They even pulled out the stove once a week to clean the floor underneath. But it didn't matter how clean and organized they kept their apartments; the uncleanliness of their surrounding neighbors still provided a limitless supply of bedbugs, mice, and an occasional cockroach to contend with, which my father would smash with his fist like a club—a clear indication of how much tougher he was than me—then mock me and Raphi when we voiced our disgust.

My mother lived in a small condo, also in Long Branch, on a street called Patten Avenue in a considerably nicer part of town. It was about two or three days after I had returned from rehab that I went to see her. I knocked on the door a few times. After waiting a minute and looking around at the condo complex, which was all new to me, I knocked a few more times. The door opened up to a goofy-looking guy who'd been in the Keswick program with me. We'll call him Dave. I had noticed my mother flirting with him on more than one occasion, and I wasn't the only one who noticed. As a matter of fact, I was brought into the office one day and asked about it by his counselor, Chaplain Freed. It was an embarrassment I didn't have a suitable response for. And now here he was—stupid smile, fake naivety, and all—greeting me as if we were long-lost friends. He had been through Keswick three times and was in his midfifties. My mother didn't really know him, though she thought she did, but I knew him, and I knew guys like him. That old saying is true: you can't hustle a hustler. He was like a leech, there to suck up whatever available resources he could and then move on to the next unsuspecting emotionally vulnerable woman.

After the initial frustrated awkwardness, we sat together on the couch while my mother was in the kitchen making coffee.

"You know who's holdin' around here?" he asked me, his eyes wide.

I laughed to myself at the situation, then got up off the couch. I didn't answer him. I ignored his questions as if he didn't exist. Then I shared an uncomfortable displeased look with my mother before walking right back out the door.

A few weeks later, some of my mother's belongings had gone missing, and I had received a phone call from my mom. Dave had invited another guy from Keswick, and the two of them had gotten ahold of some of my mother's money and spent it on a drug and alcohol binge for an entire weekend.

When I arrived at her condo that afternoon, Dave and his friend were sprawled out asleep on the couch and living room floor while my mother was at work. I'd had enough. I woke them up and took him for a walk. My Christianity was set aside in that particular moment as I tapped into the old me.

"You don't want to stay here," I told him. "This place has been nothing but trouble for me. The only people I know here are gangsters, hustlers, murderers even. You need to stay here with my mother like you need a hole in the head."

He understood and left shortly after that. I had considered staying at my mother's condo, but even after the leech had left town, I decided to stay with my father, at least for the time being.

ACROSS THE STREET FROM MY father's place was a dive bar. It looked out of place—small, dingy, run-down, and right in the middle of a residential neighborhood. I had spent the past few weeks trying to keep myself busy, reading the book of Proverbs early in the morning, as was my practice at Keswick, and attending the Armenian church on Sundays. I even attended the Armenian genocide commemoration that year in Times Square. I remember reading *Bloody News from My Friend* by Atom Yarjanian, better known by his pen name, Siamanto, on the train. I guess it was boredom, loneliness, or just a complete ignorance of how to live a normal life that made me walk in.

The bar had almost no light except for when the door opened to introduce another poor soul. During the day, it was a quiet place where a person could go to be depressed and lost about life. It was also a tiny place but with enough room for a jukebox and pool table. The mixed scent of all sorts of liquor and stale beer mingled with a variety of different cigarette brands being smoked. I sat and drank a beer, enjoying the flirty conversation with the curly-haired middle-aged bartender. The drinks relaxed me, and the conversation passed the time. I sat there thinking of myself as having a level up on everyone, that I was simply a spectator, just doing research like a journalist might do.

Until I found myself there way after midnight, and my drunken realization that I wasn't just a spectator set in. I remembered who I had always been without God's undeserved favor. In the back of the bar was a patio that looked more like a backyard barbecue. Music blared as local miscreants laughed, drank, groped one another, and slurred vulgarities. A tiny spoon of cocaine raised itself up to my nostril. I didn't think about where I was or how I'd gotten there; I had been getting high since Rich lit my first joint as a kid. It had made the abuse more bearable, somehow easier. It came as natural as breathing to snort it in one quick sniff. Then that familiar bitter taste hit the back of my throat. The numbing sensation engulfed my sinuses.

I walked out of the bar thinking about the first few verses in the book of Psalms. "Blessed is the man who walks not in the counsel of the ungodly, nor stands in the path of sinners, nor sits in the seat of the scornful; but his delight is in the law of the Lord, and in His law he meditates day and night. He shall be like a tree planted by the rivers of water, that brings forth its fruit in its season, whose leaf also shall not wither; and whatever he does shall prosper" (Psalm 1:1-3 New King James Version).

I'd found myself in this situation because I had started out walking, then I stopped for a minute and stood around for trivial conversation, and then finally, I sat down for hours. God's word is so relevant, and so began a rematch between me and the devil.

"When an evil spirit leaves a person, it goes into the desert, seeking rest but finding none. Then it says, 'I will return to the person I came from.' So it returns and finds its former home empty, swept, and in order. Then the spirit finds seven other spirits more evil than itself, and they all enter the person and live there. And so that person is worse off than before. That will be the experience of this evil generation" (Matthew 12:43-45 NLT).

Anyone who has gotten clean and gone back to addiction knows this verse is one hundred percent true.

IT HAD BEEN SIX MONTHS since I'd returned home from Keswick and taken that bump of cocaine. I sat in my cell at Monmouth County Correctional, completely strung out. My key bump of cocaine had morphed back into a habit of a bundle and a half a day. I had never been in jail for more than a few days. My uncle Jirayir, who was doing ten years of federal time in upstate New York, came to mind. I couldn't imagine how he survived. Honestly though, it felt like I had been in a cell doing time all my life. A jail cell is clean compared to the filthy spiritual prison I had been in since I was a little boy. In a real jail, locks don't sound the same. Real jail is nowhere near as dark, and there's always at least the hope of getting out. In hell, there is no such hope.

But I was back—back behind the bars, back in my shame, back in my guilt, back in that loser mentality. My inner voice of self-proclaimed victimhood felt like an old friend, reassuring me that it wasn't my fault. It wasn't my own decisions that had brought me back here; it was just in my nature, how God had made me. I loved the feeling of that excuse. It was everyone else; it was just my environment; I was a product of my own unfortunate circumstances. I must have been born this way; it must've been a disease; I was unable to do anything other than what I had done. But the truth was, it had always been me—the ugly beautiful man in the reflection, who I loved and hated at the same time. The one capable of good and evil. A man who had a heart like all men do, with God's law written on it.

A loud voice echoed through the jail. "Bible study, two minutes!"

I walked out of my cell toward the designated room, passing the other inmates, whose faces had been hardened by years of their own pain. *I'm good on the God stuff*, their faces said as they ignored the call to study what to them must have been nothing but a collection of two-thousand-year-old fairy tales. Babies born already addicted to drugs, cockroaches, bedbugs, rats, soiled commercial carpet, cursing, fighting, stabbing, gunshots, crack pipes, needles, money, sex, abortions, abuse, rape, beatings, robberies, prostitution, filthy motels, locks that didn't lock, crime scenes, yellow caution tape, bricks, bundles and bags, digital scales and bodegas, concrete and crime, weight in grams, and blurred lines between cops and gangsters—*that* had been their reality. I knew because it was mine too.

I sat at the table by myself, and the visiting pastor sat across from me in the cold room with neatly painted walls and floors with sharp edges. The space was clean, institutional, like a hospital or any other government building, with that familiar smell of industrial cleaning agent mixed with a bit of must. Bright fluorescent lights seemed to expose even the deepest parts of me. I was careful not to make eye contact, like I could hide in plain sight. The pastor looked as if he had compassion for me. If there was an exact opposite of the look I had seen on the faces of doctors, police, or the people who shooed me away when I asked them for money, an opposite of the look the Pharisees had on their faces as they looked on in disgust as Jesus ate and talked with sinners, than this was it. It was exactly the same compassionate kind of look my father had on his face when he gave money, coffee, or food to the homeless people outside of convenience stores.

Jesus, of course, understands our struggle and the human condition—what the Bible calls "the flesh"—in a way the religious man never could. The mysterious mixture of good and bad we all are, the complexities of our stories no one seems to care about.

"We'll be reading from John, chapter fourteen, starting at verse one," he said.

I riffled through the pages to find my place, making that sweet fluttering sound only the pages of the Bible can make.

"You know your Bible," the pastor said with a smile.

"Yes," I said quietly, looking down at my hands and my baggy dark green jumpsuit. *How did I get here?* I thought to myself as he started to read.

" 'Do not let your hearts be troubled.' " Those seven simple words of Jesus broke my heart, and the tears poured out of my eyes like waterfalls. The pastor never paused and kept reading over my crying. " 'You believe in God; believe also in me.' " I covered my face with my hands like a child might do. He continued. " 'In my Father's house, there are many rooms. If this were not so, would I have told you that I am going to prepare a place for you? And if I go and prepare a place for you, I will come again and take you to myself, that where I am you may be also. You know the way to the place where I am going.' " He skipped a few verses. " 'I am the way, and the truth, and the life. No one comes to the Father except through me.' "

Even after all I had done, even in that place of brokenness and addiction, if I were to have breathed my last breath, I would have been with Jesus for eternity. Once you are saved, there's nothing and no one that can take you out of His hand. I'd thought, like a lot of people do, that if my good deeds somehow outweighed my bad deeds, that was my ticket to heaven, but it is Christ's righteousness and not our own that seals our place in heaven.

It didn't matter that I had fallen again. I wasn't who the world thought I was or even who I thought I was; I was exactly who my Father said I was. And just like a father picks his child up when he stumbles and falls, Jesus picked me up and set my feet back on the ground.

The Bible reminds us that we have not yet resisted sin to the point of shedding blood. And for some reason that was at the forefront of my mind. It was as if God the Father were saying, "Come on, son. You're not bleeding yet. Get up! You can do this. Who cares what anyone says? I believe in you! Let's show 'em. Let's show 'em all!"

It has been in my deepest failures, weaknesses, and pain that I've found strength in Jesus, the one who defeated death itself when He rose up three days after they killed Him, neatly folded the clothes He had been buried in, rolled away the enormous stone with which they'd sealed the tomb, and walked out of His own grave. The good news, the Gospel message, is that even though we will all die and face judgement the moment after we breathe our last breath, and even though we're all sinners and are on our way to hell, anyone anywhere at any time—no matter what they have done or what's been done to them, regardless of who they've been—who calls on the name of the Lord with their whole heart will be saved.

It was as if God had breathed new breath into my lungs, and I was reminded of who I was in Him. But when I got out, I went right back to the needle. That black nylon belt with the silhouette of Jesus in His crown of thorns wrapped around my arm and stared up at me, reminding me of who I belonged to.

A FEW DAYS AFTER I returned home from jail, I sat in my mother's apartment on Patten Avenue in Long Branch, once again lost, once again alone, once again like a wandering sheep without a shepherd. My father stood in the open doorway in a clean white T-shirt tucked into his jeans, with his thin brown hair neatly combed. The open door allowed the bright glow of summer to shine into the darkness of the apartment. "What's going on in here?" he asked, half-serious and half-lighthearted, imitating my grandfather's heavy Armenian accent to make me smile.

"I'm dying." I plopped down on the couch. My father knew what withdrawal felt like—maybe not from heroin, but withdrawal from pills can be just as bad.

"Listen, son. I got you a spot at the Salvation Army in Brooklyn. Your uncle Michael knows a few people from when he was there."

Michael Barret was a friend of my dad's who was around all my life and had spent some time there himself.

"Only catch is, you gotta be clean for three days for them to take you."

My eyes rolled at the unrealistic expectation.

"Come with me, son. We'll spend time together, fish, hang out. I got some good *khemelik*"—pot—"and we'll smoke as much as you need. You gotta do this, Aj. It's life or death. You're gonna die out here." His voice shook. Pain contorted his face, and desperation colored his words.

I leaned my head back and put my arms behind my head, thinking about it. "Give me forty bucks to go get high one last time, and I'll go," I told him.

He unclipped the chain off his wallet and opened it up, then took out the bills he had inside.

I headed to Ridge Avenue with two twenties in hand, where I would sit at my dealer's place and shoot the last four bags of dope I'd ever shoot.

TWELFTH ROOM

BROOKLYN ZOO

SITTING IN THE PASSENGER SEAT OF MY FATHER'S van on our way to downtown Clinton Hill, Brooklyn, reminded me of all those rides we took together on late Friday afternoons when I was a kid. He'd pick me up for the weekend, and we would head an hour south to the house he rented on Mystic Island in South Jersey. The house was small, but nice and quiet with a boat docked right in the backyard. To my father, it might as well have been a mansion in the wealthy town of Rumson, New Jersey, on the Navesink River with a yacht in the back. Except now I was twenty-seven years old, a high school dropout with no job and nowhere to live, and once again a heroin addict after four months of intense Christian rehabilitation, on my way to Brooklyn, New York, to try one more time to change my life. Back to the starting line. This was life or death. My addiction had become worse than ever. I had to get this right.

The dashboard and cupholders were neat and organized, home to a pack of Marlboro Reds, the backup pack, and a silver Zippo my father must have found somewhere, along with a collection of antique model cars from the 1930s he was sure was worth a fortune. My little brother and I teased him mercilessly about the abundant inheritance we would receive one day from the treasures he'd found in other people's trash, to which my father would respond with a smirk and say, "That's it. Both of you idiots are out of the will."

An amber glass ashtray sat on top of a cupholder—a leftover relic from our family's hotel—filled with white-gray ash and crinkled cigarette butts not all the way smoked. My father's middle-aged face now focused on the road. We'd spent three days clean together so I'd be eligible for a spot at the Salvation Army, and stubble coated his jaw and cheeks. He, Raphi, and I had spent those days fishing and watching the sunset on Eighth Avenue beach. Those three days were so peaceful. The sickness from the withdrawal was somehow miraculously easy.

My father still had a full head of hair, though it was thin and carefully combed. He wore a pair of reading glasses that looked out of place on him but also made him look like an older wiser version of me. The rolled sleeves of his plaid shirt, which wasn't meant for summer, exposed his hairy forearms, and that hand, that damn hand with the scar, gripped the steering wheel. It paled in comparison to the scars on his heart that reminded me of my own scars and how similar we were.

A measuring tape and a Shaw Carpet leather-bound notebook sat on top of the dash, half-filled with carpet job diagrams and black numbers, the other half with song lyrics and scattered thoughts and ideas that were meant for packed stadiums in another life but would only be heard by me and Raphi in smoke-filled kitchens in the middle of the night. I took a cigarette out of his pack, and he looked at me with a serious face, then smiled as I smiled back. Not just anyone could take something from him without asking, but I could.

We smoked our cigarettes and talked like we had on those drives to Mystic Island when I was a kid, though about more consequential things than we did when I was seven, like life, women, love, loss, disappointments, hope, and failures—his and mine, which I was finally old enough to appreciate. We didn't need words to talk, only looks and body language, but we used them anyway—eighty percent English, fifteen percent Armenian, and five percent Turkish, as was our custom.

"*Khemelik oonees, Bub?*" I asked. *You have pot, Dad?* The words rolled off my tongue like only Armenian words could.

He looked a little annoyed, like a lion might when his cub nips at his legs. "*Nayeh,* glove compartment *een metch.*" *Look in the glove compartment.*

I lounged back in my seat and lit up the joint as we crossed over the Verrazzano-Narrows Bridge, New York's skyline in all its glory in full view. "Hey, *Bub?*" I asked, breaking the silence before I inhaled more pungent smoke. "You remember that time you made me fight that Mexican kid, Tiko, when I was like six?"

My father let out a little chuckle. "Tiko? Yeah, of course I remember. You could have had 'im too."

"Dad, he was like twelve, twice my size, and his father was a professional boxer."

"So what? He didn't even use his hands. He swept you off your feet and knocked the wind out of you!"

I smiled a little as I thought of it. "Yeah, I remember I couldn't breathe. I thought I was gonna die."

"But did you?"

I let the smoke out of my lungs and passed the joint back to him, answering at the same time. "Nah, I didn't."

"You're a tough kid, Aj. That sweep only took you down because you weren't expecting it. Street fights are like life; they don't play by the rules. You do what you gotta do to survive, and if it doesn't kill you, it'll just make you stronger. You live to fight another day, and you learn from it. If you can learn to do that, even a loss becomes a win. *Haskatsar?*"

"*Ayo gu haskenam, Bub.*"

Yeah, I understand, Dad.

I GOT OUT OF THE van and looked up at the brick building. On the corner stood a streetlight with green signs that read *Downing* and *Quincy*. The sidewalks were light gray, with spots of gum and filth and garbage littered here and there. Two large garage doors led into a warehouse where I would work and hang clothes for eight hours a day. A few guys from the program sat outside on milk crates smoking cigarettes and studying me as I kissed and hugged my father goodbye. And then in I went, like I had always been there. *Okay, Lord. It's you and me*, I thought to myself.

Brooklyn definitely gave me enough rope to hang my-self. This place wasn't Keswick.

I lived with some characters. We were in the middle of the notorious Bedford-Stuyvesant part of Brooklyn. For those who may not be familiar, it was the home of Biggie Smalls and Jay-Z. The Marcy Projects weren't too far from where I was, just down the street from the Barclays Center, which had just broken ground on its new construction. Back then, you could have put me in any hood in America and I could have found my way around. The streets are the same everywhere. I think 50 Cent said it the best in his song "I'm A Hustler" back in 2014: "Ain't nothin' changed in the game, but faces and names. The state, the weight, the date and the jake."

I snuck out onto the fire escape the first night. We were allowed to smoke, but not after lights-out. Brooklyn is like a city within a city, and anybody who's lived there knows what I'm talking about. I sat there on the half-rusted fire escape, the cool summer night breeze just enough to carry the cigarette smoke out of my mouth and nose. I watched the various activities going on down the block: cars driving back and forth, people walking up and down the street, talking, yelling, spitting, cursing, selling dope. Brooklyn has a particular smell too; car exhaust, garbage, the must-iness of the street, all the brick, pizza places, ethnic food, and smoke all make up its distinct essence.

"Yo! You ain't supposed to be out here! Ima give you one warnin', bro! You get kicked outta here fuh dat!" somebody said from the hall. I didn't know who it was, so I flicked the rest of my cigarette onto the street and watched as the glowing embers popped and exploded all over the pavement, then crawled back in through the window.

The sickness was hitting me pretty hard all of a sudden, but nothing like Keswick. I found my way to the little library, where I stayed up the rest of the night and read almost all of Lorenzo Carcaterra's novel *Gangster* in one sitting, then headed straight down to the kitchen at 5:00 a.m. It was too early for food, but a guy in the kitchen happened to be from Asbury Park, and he let me have my coffee and read my Bible for an hour before everybody else woke up and Brooklyn became a zoo.

I had an appointment with Jesus every morning at 5:00 a.m. One of those mornings, I read what is to me the greatest short story and the best news in the whole Bible. It's called the Parable of the Prodigal Son. It's about a son who went to his father and asked for his inheritance early. The father gave the young boy what he asked of him, and then he left to embark on a journey. The boy spent the money on prostitutes and alcohol. Riotous living, Jesus explained—I knew a little bit about that kind of living. He ended up broke in a country far away from his home just as a famine hit the land. Finally, he hit rock bottom. He found himself in a pigsty, so hungry he wished he could eat the slop the pigs were given. Something happened in that pigsty—maybe guilt upon the revelation of what he had become. Whatever it was, he came to his senses, and he said, "Even the servants in my father's house have bread enough to spare, and I die with hunger. I will rise and go to my father's house." He even prepared a speech and practiced what he might say.

As he got close to the house, ready to ask his father to be a servant, his father did what any father would do. He saw him a long way off and started running, as if he had been waiting every day since his son had left for him to come back home. Before the boy could say a word, his father hugged him tight, and they were both overcome with emotion. The father ordered his servants to put a ring on his finger and to get him a clean robe and shoes, and threw a party to celebrate his precious son coming home where he belonged.

Jesus goes on to explain that this is what it looks like when a sinner returns to God. I realized there in the quiet of that morning that our failures don't define us. Our pasts do not define our futures, and there is always hope, and anybody can change. If this boy came back, why couldn't I? God is the God of second and sometimes even third and fourth chances. He is gracious, full of mercy, and abounding with love. I returned to the Lord with all my heart and found Him waiting there yet again with open arms as a father for his long-lost son. I was home, I was clean, and it felt good.

It wasn't long before I got a promotion from my job sorting donated clothes to the phone room, where I took calls from people who wanted to donate all kinds of items. The room was a glass cubicle, big enough for four chairs and a few phones. The carpet was duct taped together, and the smell of freshly and strongly brewed Café Bustelo we bought in giant vacuum packs from the bodega down the street permeated the small space. Multiple voices fielded phone calls from people wanting to donate everything from clothes to unused caskets. Callers would sometimes be put on hold as the guys tried to figure out how and where the items could be fenced for cash. Everybody had a hustle—clothes, jewelry, furniture—they made extra money doing. I didn't rat anyone out, of course, but I also didn't involve myself. I was content to live off the little bit of unemployment money I had left and the eight dollars a week I made in the phone room.

I spent most of my time working out with "Frankie Deranged," an Italian kid from Bensonhurst, or getting girls' numbers on the train with Otis, a funny Black guy from somewhere in east New York who had a big heart, joked around a lot, and treated me like a brother. If I elevated my game with women during that time, it was thanks to Otis.

There was a guy named Curtis who came in a few weeks after I'd gotten there. He had just done ten years of federal prison time somewhere in upstate New York. He was over six feet and probably 250 pounds of solid muscle. He kept to himself and was tough to read because he really didn't make too many facial expressions, but he had those eyes that looked right through you. Nobody made eye contact or bothered trying to talk to him. I noticed he liked instant coffee though, and I had what must have been a pound of it in my room that I was never going to drink. We often sat in what I guess you'd call a large living room, where we'd hang out, watch movies, play pool, and eat snacks before lights-out.

One night, I saw Curtis sitting by himself. I ignored the warnings from the guys and grabbed the coffee from my room, then walked up and handed it to him. He gave me a big smile. Curtis loved me after that. He was more scared of everyone else than they were of him. Curtis and I became workout buddies.

The gym was in a basement, musty with water on the floor and a few old pieces of equipment, including rusty plates and a few dumbbells. I lost forty pounds and started building a whole new wardrobe. I was twenty-seven and in the best shape of my life, and I felt like I could conquer the world. Our curfew kept me from really being able to date, but I loved practicing pickup lines. The drugs had kept me from any real interest in women, and now that I was clean, we'll just say my interests were working over-time. But it wasn't just sexual experiences I was after; I wanted more than that. I wanted a wife, someone I could love and cherish, someone who would love me and look to me to lead her, have my back through all the strug-gles and be there to celebrate all the blessings, someone I could have babies with, start a family with, a woman to be the other half of me, someone with whom I could share every part of my life.

On a visit home, I saw a man walking with his wife on Asbury Park Boardwalk, holding her hand while pushing a stroller with a baby. They kept their eyes on their little boy as he ran ahead of them. They were all eating ice cream and enjoying what looked like a really nice day together.

A gentle whisper came into my head. "You'll never have that. You'll never be married. You'll never have a wife and kids. You'll never be a father. You're twenty-seven. You have no job, no money, no license. You owe every township money. You're on probation. You still have court cases pending! Forget it. You're a liar, a thief, a drug addict, a loser!"

But an opposite voice began to speak subtly at the same time. "I am your God. I will strengthen you; I will help you; I will uphold you with my righteous right hand. I know the plans I have for you, plans to prosper you and not to harm you, plans to give you a hope and a future. I will never leave you or forsake you. I will restore what the locusts have eaten."

One foot in front of the other, I thought. *One day, one hour, one minute at a time if I have to. I'll crawl inch by inch if that's what it takes. I'm gonna be that guy one day. I'm gonna be a daddy.*

BACK IN BROOKLYN, WE ALL gathered in the TV room, which was controlled by an old man who ruled the remote with an iron fist. Nothing but *CSI* twenty-four hours a day, seven days a week. The television shut off as everyone piled into their seats. The most mature among us shushed everybody, demanding respect for the counselor who'd come to speak, a skinny Dominican guy who wore suit pants, a shirt and tie, and a beat-up leather jacket that looked like it was from the eighties. His face was serious as he looked around the room, sizing everyone up. Finally, his mouth opened.

"Any of y'all got nicknames?"

A few guys raised their hands.

"You, go ahead!" He pointed next to me in Frankie's direction.

Frankie came from a mob-entrenched Italian neighborhood in Sheepshead Bay, and they had been calling him Frankie Deranged since he was a kid. "Yeah, dey call me Frankie Deranged," he said in his thick Brooklyn accent.

"Why they call you that? Are you deranged?"

Frankie, obviously off-put by the pointed question, said, "Nah. I mean, not really. I guess I was, uh . . . I did some crazy things when I was younger, and I don't know. It just stuck. You know what I'm sayin'?"

"Mm-hmm! So, how long have you been tryin' to live up to what they said you were? Deranged."

Frankie didn't answer.

"See, it's enough with the façade, guys. Who are you? I mean, who are you *really*? Who do you want to be? Because you could reinvent yourself starting now. Today! But are you willing to face who you really are, without the protection of that character you created for yourself all those years ago? Are you willing to let that go and move on? Are you willing to be vulnerable? Honest? True to yourself? It's time to take responsibility and take ownership."

I listened. We all listened. We knew exactly what he was asking us to do. Who was I? Really though. Without the drugs, without the wannabe gangster nonsense, without the fake tough exterior, who was I? The truth was petrifying. I was a just a lost little boy from a broken home. The one who ran back out after my dad dropped me off for a second kiss and a hug. The one who always wanted more attention from my mom. Who felt ashamed of the sex abuse and the weight I put on trying to hide so people wouldn't see the pain, weakness, anxiety, and lack of self-respect. I wanted to be loved; I wanted to be accepted; I wanted peace. I brought the truth of who I was—I mean who I *actually* was—to Jesus just like that.

Here I am, Lord. All messed up just like everyone else. A sinner.

No sugarcoating, just the bitter pill. When we take a real inventory and are soul-crushingly honest with ourselves, we can build from there. Truth as the ground floor is what skyscrapers are built on.

That same day, I was asked to come to the office. The counselor, with the phone to his ear, made fun of the conversation with his animated eyes. "Yeah . . . Yeah, I understand that . . . Mm-hmm. Yes, okay, but is there—ma'am? Ma'am? Okay, but I mean, he's doing so great here. He's even helping other guys . . . Mm-hmm, I see. Okay, well, it is what it is, I guess. I'll tell him . . . Okay, thank you. God bless. Bye-bye."

When he hung up the phone, he explained. "That was your probation officer. She insists you be on a train back to New Jersey today, or you'll be extradited back."

"*Extradited?*"

He nodded. "Yup. It's ridiculous, but that's it. You know how it is, so . . . Listen, you're doing great. You got a few months clean. Just go home and keep your nose clean, *comprende?*"

I nodded yes, but my mind was moving a thousand miles a minute, considering my next moves. I packed up my belongings and said goodbye to a few people, and before I knew it, I was in Penn Station, waiting for the train to take me back home. Home to the neighborhoods where

I sold drugs and the bathrooms and boardwalk benches where I shot dope, back to the alleys and bodegas, back to the people, back to the places, and back to the things.

On the train, I was petrified that as soon as I stepped off onto the platform, some evil force would take me over, and I'd be back to shooting dope.

The train stopped, and I stepped out and waited for that evil force, but it never showed up.

THIRTEENTH ROOM

MAY I HAVE THIS DANCE?

I WAS AWAKE IN THE DREAM I HAD WITH YOU ON THE Bosporus.

The majestic body of water unraveled east from west, the Black Sea from the Mediterranean, similar to how your body unravels pleasure, pain, light, dark, past, present, heaven, hell.

I loved the rhythm of your high heels clicking up the winding marble Ottoman steps.

A cobalt-blue dress wrapped a treasure, like a gift, given by the Almighty.

The ghosts of this place seemed to rise up off the glimmering black water, not haunting me, but rather coming to my aid. The presence of angels visited me from ancient history.

Ermeni, Ermeni, Ermeni, biz Ermeniyiz.

Armenian, Armenian, we are Armenian, the voice whispered. Something deep, deep in my blood cried out from the ground. Something as strong as a son of steel, Demirjian, saying with a sweet cadence, *Kiss her, hold her, cherish her, kiss her like I was kissed and cherished when I was young so many years ago.*

Here on the Bosporus.

Aferim yavris. Eat, smoke, drink, laugh, cry, sing, fight, dance, make up, make love forever, make life. Love her like I was loved before I died, while our great-grandparents lie here at peace here on the Bosporus. Focus on the light of the young woman's eyes, look way down, through the windows, see the soul.

As you fall in love with her where I once fell in love long ago.

I gave myself away in some distant memory, and I'm happy I did.

Feel present, exist here and now, and walk away hand in hand from this place with your bride. Walk away and don't look back, just as we did, here on the Bosporus.

I THOUGHT THAT POEM UP one night while looking at my wife during our honeymoon in the late summer of 2015. She sat there across from me at a restaurant on the Bosporus in Istanbul. Her eye shadow and black mascara made her big eyes appear even bigger and more beautiful. We were thrilled by the thought of starting our life together. We were falling even deeper in love with each other, just like my grandparents had fallen in love on that waterfront so many years ago.

We'd found ourselves in a different world. In her cobalt-blue dress, with her tan skin and almost-black hair, she posed on the shiny marble steps in the former Turkish palace that had no doubt hosted prominent figures, such as Turkish royalty and Armenian dignitaries and foreign diplomats in Ottoman times. I was overwhelmed by the architecture designed by Armenian architects like the famous Balyan family.

How had I gotten here? It felt like a dream. I should not have been newly married to the girl of my dreams, traveling to mystical places like Mykonos, Santorini, or Istanbul. I should not have been holding hands with her, walking on cobblestone streets, sipping champagne, and laughing. I should not have been enjoying warm summer nights in our hotel room.

I should have been dead.

But here we were, in the place where my grandparents had grown up. Lights reflected off the water, and the beautiful night sky stretched above us, accented with millions of stars. The soft glow of the moon over the Bosporus blanketed the random boats coming and going, merchants buying and selling, and ships docking and departing. I could imagine my grandfather flirting with the young girl at her family's Armenian restaurant. I could imagine her shy but curious smile, while her parents were wary of the young boy, who was as handsome as a movie star and spoke as smoothly as oil. With his slicked-back hair, olive skin, and perfect mustache, my grandfather grew up as a hustler in a world that connected trade between Europe and Asia. Maybe there was some of that in me.

I couldn't help but think of all the history in this place that had made my grandfather leave his wife and children behind in Turkey to start a new life in a new country before saving enough money to bring them over with him. It was the genocidal attitude toward Armenian Christians and the strangeness of being an Armenian in Istanbul that lives on even now. That attitude; that denial of the brutal reality of genocide; that rewriting of history; that Turkish theft of artifacts, architecture, money, jewelry, rugs, and generational wealth; that lack of trust for Armenian Turks was what ultimately led me to be who I am and where I was at that very moment—an Armenian American back where we all started on the Bosporus with my wife, looking at the exact same view through a different lens.

I don't know what it was about her standing in front of me on the dance floor the night we first met five years earlier. The dim colorful lighting made her bright pink dress stand out in a way that highlighted how perfectly it matched my tie. Her dress was classy but formfitting, and her playful smile drew me in as she tried to talk over the loud music and busyness of the wedding. In that moment, everyone else and all the hustle and bustle faded into the background, and all I could see was her. Her voice had a throatiness to it that I found extremely sexy, and her perfume had a subtle sweetness that made me weak.

If she hadn't started dancing with me, I would have left much earlier. I noticed her when I first walked in. I also noticed her noticing me. I had a lot on my mind back then, and I know I always looked serious. I was friendly but gave off an obvious lack of interest in meeting anyone. But I guess it must have been the right type of mysterious—

maybe the kind of mysterious that makes a woman need to be noticed by a man.

It had been a busy year since I'd gotten home from Brooklyn. It was my longest period without drugs since I was eleven years old, and I was working three jobs to pay off my fines. I reported to every probation appointment early and met every obligation of my mandatory Narcotics Anonymous meetings. Every one of my court cases was wrapped up, and I had gotten my license back. I had also gone to Brookdale Community College and against all odds had earned my high school diploma. I'd had more successes in that year than I'd had in the fifteen years prior.

But there was something really significant missing in my life. I was alone. It wasn't good, and I felt it. I had met many women since I'd been home, but very few of them held my attention for long, and even fewer of them were able to make me even consider commitment. One of those girls had left her boyfriend for me. We worked together at a restaurant in a beach town called Sea Bright, but it turned out to be just a fling, and she had gone back to her boyfriend right before the wedding. She was supposed to be my date. I'd already learned to never expect too much from people. That way, when they let you down—and they will— at least you won't be surprised.

I almost didn't get the chance to attend the wedding that night. I had reached out to my best friend, whose wedding it was, after getting home from Brooklyn and got no answer. When you mess up and take advantage of the people closest to you like I did for so long, eventually they find their limit. I received a return voicemail letting me know I shouldn't bother calling again, among a few other choice words. I heard his voice, and I listened to it carefully. It was my job to listen to what I had done to people, and for the next few years, I was reminded over and over who I used to be. It was a part of the process. I understood that.

I called back and left another voicemail, telling him, "I understand if you don't believe me, but this time is different, and I'd love to tell you why, to show you. If you ever want to talk, just know I'm here."

I didn't hear anything right away, but I prayed about it. He called me back a few weeks later and told me he wanted me to come to the wedding. So there I was, a year clean, trying to make up for a lifetime of failure, feeling happy for my friend while simultaneously wondering if I would ever have what I'd always wanted: a family of my own.

But back to her bright pink dress. I began to dance as we leaned into each other to ask questions.

"What's your name?"

"Aj," I told her. "What's yours?"

"Nicole," she answered. "Come here. Take a picture," Nicole said to her friend as she wrapped my arms tight around her body. "We're going to Bar A after this, in Belmar. You should come!" She moved her body to the music, smiling and holding my hands while we danced.

I know it sounds stupid, but I couldn't help but notice her hands. Nicole had the most beautiful hands, with perfectly manicured French tips, and they looked good in mine.

"Try to stop me," I said as cool as I could manage.

She wrote her number on a piece of paper that I folded and put in the inside pocket of my suit jacket as I walked away. I was a little upset about the girl that had ditched me before the wedding, and I hadn't been interested in meeting anyone, but all I could think about on the way to Belmar was the cute girl in the bright pink dress.

I pulled into the jammed-up parking lot at Bar Anticipation. I waited as the phone rang over and over again, finally going to a voicemail. I tried again. Still no answer. Normally, I would have just gone home, but I was kind of annoyed that I had wasted so much time and energy driving over there. I walked into the bar, where the music blasted and I was elbow to elbow with drunken college kids. It was like a bad episode of *Jersey Shore*. The smell of cheap cologne, perfume, and alcohol paired appropriately with the festivity of the Fourth of July weekend.

I looked over most of the crowd and in a few different rooms and couldn't find Nicole. I was just about to leave when I spotted her standing with her back to me. As I walked closer, she reached up to cover her eyes. Tears streamed down her face. She looked pitiful standing there alone in that crowd of rowdy people. Everything in me wanted to protect her.

"Hey, hey, don't cry," I said when I was close enough to be heard. "What's wrong?"

"Nothing. I'll be okay." But she wasn't okay. She'd had a run-in a few minutes earlier with her ex-boyfriend, and they'd had a fight when she saw him with another girl.

I took her hands away from her face once she gave up trying to keep them there and held them as I looked into her eyes. "You wanna get outta here?" I asked with a smile.

She looked up at me and nodded.

Hand in hand, we walked through the crowd out into the summer night.

"You wanna come home with me?" I asked.

"I'm not like that!" she said. "I don't go to a guy's house the first night we meet."

"Okay, okay." I laughed. "So, where you wanna go?"

"We can go to my parents' house if you want, but just to talk," Nicole said with a stern face.

"Okay, let's go."

We walked a few blocks to her parents' house and sat outside on the bench in her backyard. I really tried to pay attention to the conversation, but I found myself repeatedly looking down at her perfectly polished toes peeking through her high heels and her legs, which were draped across mine while we talked for hours. I met her mother, her brother, and her sister when they made their appearances one by one throughout the night. I could tell they were surprised I was there.

We talked until 4:30 in the morning. I remember the time because I didn't want to be late for work, and by that time, both of us had fallen pretty hard. From that night forward, we were inseparable.

❧

NICOLE LAY IN OUR BED with a white comforter wrapped around her. A cold blank stare had overtaken her face, and I racked my brain for what to say. We had just gone through a miscarriage, and I was desperate to help. I had been listening to a pastor on the radio named Bill Beckelman from Calvary Chapel Coastlands in Eatontown, New Jersey, not far from where we lived.

I took a shot and asked her, "Would you want to go to church?"

Nicole didn't say anything, but she got up and started to get dressed.

After the church service, we sat together at a dark brown table with Pastor Bill and his wife, Candice, telling them a bit about ourselves and our situation.

Pastor Bill asked us plainly, "So, are you two living together?"

We looked at each other. "Yes, of course."

"But you're not married?" Pastor Bill asked, as if to state the obvious problem.

"No, but we're engaged," Nicole said.

"How long have you been together?"

"Four years," we said.

"So, what are you waiting for?"

"Well, I just want to make sure we're right for each other, I guess," Nicole said.

"He's not a pair of shoes, dear."

Nicole blinked rapidly, and she cleared her throat, clearly surprised by the bluntness of his response.

"Everyone has flaws. We're all sinners. Marriage is

about helping each other become more like Jesus and about supporting each other through the trials of life, regardless of our flaws and the disappointments. No one is exactly right for each other, at least in that sense," he explained.

We continued to study through the book of Genesis, learning about the first marriage between Adam and Eve. Adam had looked all over the earth for a suitable helper, but none was found. So God caused Adam to fall into a deep sleep, and He took Adam's rib—which Pastor Bill explained was the Hebrew word for *side*—and from Adam's side, God made Eve and brought her to Adam.

"And Adam said, 'Whoa, man!' " Pastor Bill exclaimed, then chuckled.

"So, what should we do?" I asked.

"Move out," he said plainly. "Repent for your sin. Be sorry for it. And move out until you get married. Stop playing house, and stop playing with fire. God will never bless this relationship as long as you're living in sin."

We left the church, confused about what we should do, but one thing was for sure: moving out was not happening. There were just too many variables. We both wanted to do the right thing though, so we decided to get married a week from that day. Just us and God against the world. We would sleep in separate rooms for the next week. It was our way of communicating to God that we were serious about the decision we'd made.

Standing at that altar with Nicole brought my life completely into focus. I saw her, really saw her, for exactly who she was—that girl standing alone in the bar, alone just like I was, scared and disappointed, always looking for love but never finding it—and all I wanted to do was protect her and provide for her. To love her. I had never been more sure of anything in my life.

We planned another wedding six months later with all the bells and whistles. Among our guests was a detective who had surveilled me with a narcotics unit and threatened to throw me off the bridge if he got stuck with a needle. I marveled at the smile on his face during the reception as he urged me to sing.

"Sing, sing!" he said enthusiastically.

I did sing—"Can't Take My Eyes off You."

No one will ever know, I thought to myself. *No one will ever truly be able to understand what it is to be me and to make it through what I've been through.*

I soaked in all the people there that night, all the smiles and the celebration. But the moment that trumped them all was my wife walking down that aisle with her father, Eddie Kirschenbaum. Years earlier, he had been part of a tactical narcotics team in the same neighborhood I'd run around in, and he was about to hand his oldest daughter to me in marriage. It doesn't happen every day that a narcotics officer gives his daughter away to a guy with my history, but that is the kind of impossible thing God does. I was grateful for his blessing and the trust he put in me that day, knowing my past and trusting me to love her.

I had never in my entire life seen anything as beautiful as my wife in her wedding dress. She was somehow mine forever. I didn't deserve any of it.

The contrast between the investigation, arrest, and eventual scuffle between me and three cops over a forced strip search in the police station and that very same detective sitting at my wedding as my guest was invisible to everyone except me. I stood in awe of God as my bride smiled at me.

NOT LONG AFTER OUR HONEYMOON and another miscarriage three months along, I heard God's voice echo through my head as I read Genesis 1:28: "God blessed them and said to them, 'Be fruitful and multiply.' " That verse had come up three times in two days from different sources. Jesus said, "My sheep hear my voice." I had learned to listen when God spoke, and I knew what He was saying.

Our last appointment with the fertility doctor left Nicole in tears. I had never been a fan of the idea, but we'd had three miscarriages by then, and the last had left my wife absolutely broken. I would've done anything if it meant having a baby with her.

"How long do you think before we can try?" my wife asked with anticipation as the doctor typed something into his computer.

"Oh, at least a year," he said. "Maybe a little more."

Nicole's face fell.

"I've outlined some of what we need to do before we can seriously think about you trying again." The doctor noticed her tears then. "Hey, listen," he said calmly, "you're very high-risk. We have to be thorough, but you'll be okay. Don't worry. This is our thing. It's what we do."

There it was, God's voice: "Pregnancy is my thing. It's what I do."

My mind was made up.

After we left the doctors' office, I told her what I believed God had said.

"Honey, I think God wants us to take the doctors out of the equation," I said with a serious look.

"Take the doctors out? What do you mean? We have a whole year's worth of appointments."

"I have a really strong feeling God is telling us to do it."

Nicole didn't like the idea. But the verse kept coming up—"be fruitful and multiply."

A few days later, we sat together in the church parking lot after Sunday service. We had spoken to our pastor and other close friends about what I felt God was telling us to do.

"Do you feel a little more comfortable about canceling the fertility doctor?" I asked.

"No, I don't," Nicole said, much to my surprise. "Maybe I'm just not meant to be a mother." Fresh tears welled in her eyes.

My heart broke as I wrestled with the idea that maybe I wasn't meant to be a father. All I had ever wanted to be since I was a little boy was a daddy. But I kept it inside as I tried to be strong for Nicole. "Let's pray one more time together right now. We'll ask God to make it so clear that we have no confusion at all. If He speaks to us, we will call the doctor Monday and cancel the entire series of appointments and put it in God's hands, but if He doesn't, I'll go with you as long as you want."

Nicole dried her tears with a tissue, and we kissed each other, then prayed together, holding each other's hands, expecting in faith to get a clear answer from God before Monday.

We were pulling out of the church parking lot when I remembered there was a Trader Joe's across the street from the church that we had been meaning to go to but hadn't yet gotten the chance. "Hey, let's go check out that Trader Joe's across the street."

"No, I just want to go home," she said. "I'm exhausted."

"Come on. Let's go! We'll be quick," I promised.

Nicole nodded, and we headed across the street. The double automatic doors opened up, and our eyes widened in disbelief. Our fertility doctor stood there with a smile. Nicole and I looked at each other, knowing what needed to be done. Our faith was a little stronger than it had ever been. We canceled the appointments in person that day and never looked back.

Two weeks later, my wife greeted me at the door after a hard day's work with a positive pregnancy test and a smile from ear to ear. We hugged each other tight, laughing and basking in the warmth of God's goodness.

"I think it's important for him to have your name if it's a boy," Nicole said.

Arman Anthony Kaymakcian Jr.

I was going to be a daddy.

FOURTEENTH ROOM

PEACHES

THE BLUE SKY WAS DRAPED WITH WHITE CLOUDS, and it looked beautiful through my windshield. I drove my dump truck home from the new construction site while I sipped a hot cup of coffee. My fleece-lined blue-checkered flannel retained the heat and kept my body warm. The smell of hot asphalt mixed with the scent of the dusty truck interior. My dirty callused hands had cracked from the cold January weather. I had nicked my hand while I was working, and the cut, positioned just next to the calluses, was still bleeding a little bit. I had seen my father's hands look just as beat-up so many times. I smiled at how I'd become as tough as he was and was so grateful in that moment, loving the quiet winter morning, warmed by God's company. I looked up at the clouds and thought of God and how good He was. I thought of all the prayers He had answered over the years. I thanked Him in my heart as I began to pray.

"Lord, I know this isn't important to anyone except

me, but I've been reading and hearing about Armenia my whole life. Nobody in my family is interested in going, and my wife doesn't really want to go. I don't even know who I would go with or how it would be possible. But if you could make a way for me, I would be so grateful. I'm asking in your name, Lord Jesus, amen."

I took another sip of the coffee and placed the expectation of an answer to my prayer somewhere far away in the back of my mind. My wife was pregnant with our first son, Arman Jr., and many of my thoughts were centered around the hope I had for his arrival. I had dreamed of being a father my entire life, but so much of my life had moved me further and further away from that reality.

A couple months passed, and I forgot all about my prayer for Armenia. I looked out at the clouds through my windshield on my way home from work and started to pray. Then I noticed something strange in the clouds—what looked like a white mountain range set in the midst of the blue horizon. It was vague yet at the same time one of the clearest things I had ever seen.

MAY, the sky said.

Those three letters were written there, seemingly smeared across the sky by the very finger of God Himself. I picked up the phone to call the person I first thought of when something interesting happened to me: my wife, best friend, and the only person who knows me almost as well as I know myself—and in some ways even better.

"Honey?"

"Yeah, what's up, babe?"

"This is so strange, but I was praying just now, and all of a sudden, I saw the word *MAY* written in the clouds."

"May?"

"Yeah, May."

"Is it good or bad?" she asked.

"Definitely good. Something very good is going to happen in May."

Nicole chuckled a little bit. "Okay, honey. Well, I guess we'll just have to wait and see."

I sensed a slight indifference in her voice, as if she couldn't quite understand the magnitude of what I was experiencing.

A few months later, I was sitting in a car in Manhattan for work when Nicole called me out of the blue.

"I want you to call your grandfather today," she said.

"Okay, why?" I asked.

"I don't know. He's getting older, and you're in the city, and his store is there. I have a strange feeling. Just call him."

I hung up the phone and dialed my grandfather's number. No answer. One minute later, I got a call back. He didn't even say hello.

"I'm going to Yerevan," he said in his thick accent.

Yerevan is the capital of Armenia. My grandfather was a jeweler and would go to different jewelry shows from time to time. I was actually annoyed at first. *Now he's gonna get to go, and I'm not gonna get to*, I thought to myself.

My next words fell right out of my mouth. "Oh, good. I'll go with you." I said it partly wishing I could go, but knowing I couldn't, completely as a joke. Nicole was a little more than three months pregnant with our first son; there was no way I could travel.

"Good, *chojukus*! I want you to go with me!"

I couldn't believe what I'd heard. I hadn't always been as close with my grandfather as I would have liked. There seemed to be this disconnect. Maybe it was generational, or maybe it was the complicated relationship he had with my father, but more than likely, it was cultural, and even more likely, it was a mixture of all three. In any case, I called my wife back immediately.

"Honey, you'll never believe this."

"Believe what?" Nicole asked.

"You're a gypsy!" I said, laughing at her psychic suggestion for me to make the call. "My grandfather is going to Armenia, and he wants me to go with him."

"Oh my gosh! Are you serious?"

"Yes!" I told her.

"You have to go," she said, surprising me.

"No, no, honey. I couldn't leave you. You're pregnant!"

"Aj! Your grandfather is ninety years old. When are you ever gonna have a chance like this again? I'm fine! Seriously! I have my mom and my sister. You have to go. Call him back."

I hung up and called my grandfather. "Grandpa, you'll never believe this, but I'm actually going with you. When are we leaving?"

"May 1, *chojukus*. We'll leave on May 1."

The word in the clouds that day had been a promise from God. He answered my prayer and gave me the experience of a lifetime. God had heard my voice once again.

❪

MY UNCLE JIRAYIR HAD FINISHED his ten-year sentence in federal prison and was now living in Armenia since his deportation back to Turkey. My grandfather had decided we would stay with him during our trip. My uncle and I had been very close when I was growing up. I guess there are a few different terms you could've used to describe him back in the day: street guy, wise guy, tough guy. I just called him Uncle Elvis.

He wasn't always around, but when he was, he had wads of cash in his pocket, was well-dressed, and talked like he owned the world. He was tall and good-looking, had curly jet-black hair, and walked with a swagger. I'd never seen my father scared of anyone in his life, but even he treaded a little lightly around his older brother. I once watched Uncle Elvis fight almost the entire Asbury Park police force one summer night, like that scene in the police station in *Rambo*.

When he wasn't around, they would tell stories about him that sounded like this: "One time, that nut made me drive him somewhere in New York and told me to lie down in the back seat with a shotgun until he came back."

Or: "Remember that time he let that giant biker talk trash to him at the bar and then followed him into the bathroom at the end of the night, smashed his face against the urinal, and left him in a puddle of blood and piss?"

Someone would reply: "Oh yeah. Elvis is crazy. They don't make 'em like him anymore."

"He's an old-time gangster."

"Yup, last of the Mohicans, that dude," they'd say.

My uncle was the kind of guy that would make his fingers into a gun, point it at the driver, and whisper, "Bang," when we passed an armored truck. But he was also the uncle who showed up from time to bring me dollars and coins from foreign countries, the guy who spoke five languages fluently, and the one who bought me and the rest of the poor Black and Hispanic kids on my block ice cream on hot summer days. He'd watch wrestling with me and take me swimming at the Sixth Avenue beach. I was like his shadow.

He left when I was about ten years old. He went on the lam, running from a conspiracy charge. I hadn't seen him since we visited him years earlier in Valhalla, New York, sometime during the start of his bid. I was a teenager then, and I remember him in his bright orange jumpsuit being brought out in handcuffs as my father started to cry.

"Come on, man. Don't cry. Don't give 'em the satisfaction," he'd said in Armenian, talking about the guards.

I remember asking, "What did you say, Uncle?"

"You don't speak Armenian?"

I lowered my head. "Not really."

"You gotta learn it, man," he'd replied. That was the day I started to get serious about learning Armenian on my own.

I had never really gotten the chance to get close to my grandfather, though I had made a few attempts. Being alone on the plane with him reminded me of being on the train in Manhattan during the week or so I spent with him when I was nine years old. He'd sent me up and down Forty-Seventh Street to deliver little manilla envelopes to men with long beards and long curls growing from underneath their black hats.

When I got back, he asked, "You know what was in that envelope?"

"What?" I asked, my eyes wide with anticipation.

"Ten tousand dollar vurth of diamonds." He smiled as I walked away feeling like James Bond.

It was tough to connect with him at that age, but here we were all these years later, my grandfather at ninety and me at thirty-two, drinking scotch and talking about life. It was basically an interview. I asked him about his parents and relatives, for stories from his childhood and teenage years. *I'll use some of this for a novel*, I thought as I fired out question after question and he rattled off answer after answer.

My grandfather had nicely combed silver hair and a handsome tan face void of most of the wrinkles a ninety-year-old would usually have. His diamond cross showed through the unbuttoned part of his dress shirt, and a gold watch, bracelet, and yellow diamond pinky ring adorned his hands, which he waved around as he told me stories. A big smile came across his face as he thought of another one.

"My brother," he said, shaking his head, surely about to tell a gem. "He was so cheap! When my parents die, we knew he's not going to travel to their funeral. So my brothers and I came up with a great idea. We call him and say, 'Listen, we found a wooden box. It's locked. We don't know what's in it. And we don't want to open until we're all together.' So he traveled an entire day to see what's in the box.'" My grandfather laughed, and I took a sip of my scotch, waiting to hear the end of the story. "He came and broke the lock to see what's inside, and it was empty! Oh, Arman! You should have seen his face! It was priceless!" He let out a few more laughs so hard that he coughed.

Much of our time on the plane was spent telling stories and making each other laugh. We enjoyed every minute of it. And I felt more comfortable with him than I ever had.

WE SAT AT A TABLE in a place called Garni, where the pagan temple stood with its large stone pillars, the last evidence of the absence of Christianity in this ancient land. I began feeling guilty that my wife wasn't there. But maybe after the lifetime of pain, it was okay to enjoy the sprawling green mountains accented with tiny bursts of bright yellow and purple flowers that sprung out of the ground like royalty and to take in the majestic views of Garni at a table heaped with lavash with my father's father. I was intent on connecting with the place many fathers had come before me as I prepared to finally be a father myself.

And so we traveled the stone walkways into the Geghard Monastery, with its mysterious ancient creatures carved into the structures, our voices echoing as we pointed them out to each other, and we drove hours into the mountains toward the Tatev Monastery, located on the edge of a high cliff. We enjoyed local cheese and wine, fresh herbs, and farm-raised lamb over apricot wood coals in the beautiful spring weather. We lit candles for our loved ones during the Divine Liturgy at Etchmiadzin, with its ancient hymns, beautiful ornate symbolism, and fragrant incense,

built in the third century. We visited Khor Virap, where the
man who'd introduced Armenians to Christianity had been
locked in a pit, which I crawled into and walked around
in. We walked through Tsitsernakaberd, the Armenian
Genocide Memorial complex, and cried together, feeling
the unending pain of the enormous evil that had been done
a hundred years earlier. Here, we shared the realization that
we had something in common that rose above generational
and cultural misunderstandings between a grandfather
and grandson. What seemed like miles of apricot trees and
grape vines Mount Ararat, where Noah's ark landed after
the Flood, graced the picturesque sky. I had to remember
that God had brought me here. It had been a long hard
road, and though I missed my wife, maybe it was okay for
me to finally live in this moment and smell the flowers that
were around every corner.

THE THREE OF US SAT at the café downstairs from my uncle's apartment on Komitas Avenue in Yerevan, one of the
oldest inhabited cities in the world remade into a string
of modern Parisian-style cafés. The quiet busyness of the
morning passed us by as I petted a tiny street dog on his
belly, kissed his face, and fed him fresh *gata*, an Armenian
sweet bread, from the bakery down the street. The locals
smiled at me as they passed. We smoked a hookah at the
café as they prepared breakfast, exhaling the grape-fla-
vored smoke from our mouths and nostrils before passing
it on. My grandfather corrected my Armenian as I tried to
pronounce the word for grapes.

"*Ghaghoghner*," he said carefully, annunciating the difficult soft *gh* sound.

We sipped Armenian coffee out of small demitasse cups with *kaymak* on top, a Turkish word used to describe a thick cream, and which is also part of our last name.

Just after the fall of the Ottoman Empire, Kemal Atatürk was hell-bent on a Turkification of the newly founded republic. In addition to largely erasing Armenian history and stealing ancient Armenian artifacts and structures and passing them off as "ancient Turkish history," he put into place what were known as surname laws, which forced Armenians to change their Armenian names to Turkish-sounding ones as well as forcing them to speak only Turkish. Our name was changed from Partamian to Kaymakcian.

My grandfather told us about how he and his friends used to smoke hash out of hookahs when he was a teenager and roast *kufteh*, Armenian spiced and herbed hamburgers, over an open fire, wishing the moment would never have to end. The sun felt good on my face as we laughed together about old stories and all the fun we'd had on our trip.

We had gotten home late the night before, and there were no lights in the stairwell to my uncle's apartment. I'd walked my grandfather carefully up the three flights, and just before we opened the door, he put his hand on the back of my neck and said, "I love you, Arman."

I had never heard that from him before, and I felt for the first time that maybe there was some wisdom in the scarcity of that phrase from him to me; it was sweeter, more meaningful, a carefully crafted phrase in a very special moment in time that most likely was not by accident. The experience with my grandfather somehow, in a way I can't quite explain, helped to prepare me for the task of fatherhood I was about to take on.

My uncle and I had stayed up late most nights taking advantage of the time and catching up on the events of the last twenty years, which were far too detailed to share in our regular letters to each other. I wished my father could have been there, but he was in no condition.

Since I had gotten clean, he'd spiraled completely into heroin addiction, and the deadly mixture of heroin and methamphetamine he did one night had caused a massive stroke, leaving him mostly unable to walk and almost completely unable to move the left side of his body. It was one of—if not the—darkest periods of his life, and at the same time, it was one of the brightest periods in mine. I felt guilty for all the good things that were happening in my life, and I wished I could have been more of a comfort to him.

Maybe it was a special ability of my father's—or maybe it was simply a father's connection to his son—that gave him the capacity to comfort me during the darkest times of my life. Or maybe it was an innate Armenian ability to mourn with those around him, cultivated by generations of mourning. I'd always wondered why it was that my family was so readily able to sympathize and connect during sadness and disappointment but almost wholly unable to celebrate and enjoy moments of success and happiness.

Maybe we're too good at mourning, I thought. *Or maybe we're not good enough.*

❧

MY GRANDFATHER LAY IN BED in his apartment in Asbury Park, his body now frail and mostly immobile. It had been a year since we'd taken our trip, during which I had used every opportunity I had to urge my grandfather to make sure he put his trust and faith in Jesus. We had gotten very close since then, talking almost every day. We had become good friends.

By this time, I was basking in the glory of being a new father. After a lifetime of dreaming about it, I had finally become a daddy. Some of the greatest gifts I have are pictures of my grandfather holding my son Arman, his great-grandson. As my son entered into this world, my grandfather was exiting it.

The apartment was quiet, with sun beaming through the windows and the distinct smell of my grandfather's cologne in the air. Coffee and pastries sat on the table, and Persian rugs lay on the floor, cushioning my son's little knees, similar to the rugs that had cushioned my father's knees in Montreal at that age and similar to the ones in Asbury Park that had cushioned mine. We helped my father into bed with my grandfather, and he held him and cried like a little boy.

What will this be like for me? I thought. *When I lose my father? What will it be like for my son when I die?*

I walked out onto the balcony to get some fresh air and looked across to the Berkeley-Carteret as a flock of seagulls flew through the sky. I'd thought that hotel was a castle when I was a kid, and my father had pretended it was, embracing my imagination. It was the same hotel where my uncle had committed suicide over a girl named Sandy that he and my father were both in love with.

I thought about life and death, about heaven and hell, about life's purpose, about salvation in Jesus. I looked in through the storm door at my son crawling around on the floor and thought about what kind of man he would be. Then I walked back in and did my best to come up with just the right words to explain to my grandfather how God wanted his heart.

He looked at me and said, "Not only my heart, but my mind and my soul as well."

I knew in that moment that I would see him again.

"Grandpa, can you hear me?" I got no response. With tears in my eyes and my voice shaking, I said, "I want you to know that our trip together was one of the greatest times in my life, and I'll never forget it."

He mustered up the strength to smile.

I asked him, "If you could have anything in the world, what would it be?"

"*Deghzner.*" *Peaches.* He made a sucking noise with his lips as if he were tasting them. "*Shad anoush eh,*" he said as he fell asleep. *They are so sweet.*

I brought back every variety of peach I could find. I don't know that he was ever actually able to taste them the way he wanted to, but what I do know is that now in mid-June when the peaches are ripest in New Jersey, every bite I take reminds me of my grandfather. How deceptive this life is—an entire lifetime of experiences, and in the end, after chasing so much of what this life has to offer, the only things that matter are your family being close as eternity approaches and the simple sweetness of a juicy peach.

The next day, he was gone. And in the months that followed, I often visited his grave at that quiet point where night meets day. One night I had gone to his grave, and a mysterious deer stood behind the stone, his eyes open wide, large antlers on full display. As I remembered my grandfather and stared at my name etched in the stone, I wrote:

How the grave stood still,
black with shimmering gold.
At twilight,
crickets played their song like an orchestra.
Glints of light from the headlights reflected off the shining
font.
I stared at my name permanently etched in the dark finality of the marble.
How the deer stood still
behind the stone,
his antlers
branched out in a large wild display,
his eyes open with fear
as one who breathed his last
while the soul escaped into eternity.
How the wind ruffled the oak leaves and swayed the shaking collection, dancing back and forth to a beautiful breezy rhythm.
I can taste the purple like velvet royalty,
the sweetness and the depth of the wine from Vayots Zor.
As the history from this place runs down my throat,

*I can see your smile, and the thin glass clinks and the day
fades.*

*I hear the singing song of the mountains dressed in yel-
low.*

The sound of the violin drags across my heart.
While the spring lamb chars over the apricot coals
and the smoke from the nargileh exhales,
I remember you here at the stone.

*A pair of empty slippers that sit by themselves, an apart-
ment without the man, a gold watch without a wrist.*

Don't tell me about time
at the stone with the name that will someday be mine
here at the stone at twilight.

FIFTEENTH ROOM

LIVING THE DREAM

OUR HOUSE WAS QUIET IN THE SUMMER OF 2018. Pictures of our family and signs that said things like *Bless This Home with Love and Laughter* and *As for Me and My House, We Will Serve the Lord* hung on our white walls, evidence of my wife's touch on our Christian home. My son Arman was eighteen months old. He sat on my lap and laughed with me while we waited for Nicole, his curious eyes big and round and the hints of gold in his brown hair becoming noticeable in the sunlight, like an angel's hair. His two prominent front teeth made me smile, along with his full cheeks and tiny arms, hands, and feet.

Nicole was almost six months pregnant, and we had already named him Nikos. We headed out for a routine appointment. We had already been to so many. I'd taken the day off work, and we planned to go to lunch in the city afterward.

My wife reclined on the blue exam table as the nurse squirted clear liquid onto her belly for the ultrasound. She moved the wand slowly back and forth, pressing it in a little to get a clearer picture. I worked hard to keep Arman occupied while also paying attention.

While we waited for the doctor, surrounded by white walls and the shiny gray floor, my eyes lingered on the red garbage bin that read *Biohazard*, the distinct hospital smell taking me back to my many attempts at rehab.

"Look at his face, babe," Nicole said, snapping me back to the present.

I studied the somewhat vague but still clearly visible outlines of his mouth and nose. The umbilical cord giving life to him was a bit of a nuisance to me since it was blocking my view. "He's gonna be a good-looking dude! That's for sure," I said, trying to ignore how much time had passed since the nurse had left the room.

"What's taking them so long?" Nicole's look of annoyance became worry, then panic.

I worked hard to hide my nervousness. "I don't know. They're probably just double-checking everything."

Tears welled up, and a look of terror overtook her eager eyes. I had seen that look before during our last miscarriage. It was a look specific only to a pregnant mother.

I left Nicole in the room, still in her hospital gown. Her legs and socked feet dangling there made her look even more vulnerable somehow. I walked back to an office where I saw the doctor and the nurse discussing something with concerned looks.

"Doc, you gotta tell us something. My wife is a wreck. Is he . . . ?"

"No, no, he's alive," he said, putting down the paperwork

in his hand. He asked for me to have Nicole get dressed and then to meet him in his office.

Nicole sobbed as she put her clothes on, preparing for what would no doubt be devastating news. I held Arman in my arms as we headed toward the back office, kissing his tiny face. He looked up at me with that innocent smile, and I was even more grateful for him than I had been a half hour earlier.

Once we were seated, the doctor took a deep breath. "Okay, so we have detected a defect in the spine. We suspect it is a form of spina bifida, but we need to get you to a specialist in order to confirm it."

We had a million questions, and we rattled them off in between Nicole crying and me trying to comfort her. Arman played with some small statues on the desk. His smile, happy eyes, and playful attitude made it perfectly clear that he was wholly unaware of the blow our family had just been dealt.

WE WERE SENT TO A specialist to confirm Nikos's condition. My father-in-law, Eddie, sat with us across from the doctor. She was an older woman, sort of overweight, with short dark hair and a mean-looking face.

"We have to do an amniocentesis," she said. Her hands pressed together at the fingertips atop her large desk. Her arrogance and casualness overwhelmed me as she explained the procedure. "We will use a syringe long enough to pierce the stomach and enter the uterus in order to extract a sample from the amniotic sac."

Oh, that's all? I thought to myself, but what I said was, "So, just to reiterate, you want to take a needle and inject it into my wife's stomach so you can pierce the amniotic sac?"

"Yes."

"And forgive me, but the amniotic sac is what God put there to protect the baby?" I asked.

She rolled her eyes at my mention of God, as if the thought of God having anything to do with babies or pregnancy was a ridiculous and outdated concept that had no place in her medical office. "Sir, we do many of these per week. I can assure you it's safe and very necessary."

"Why exactly is it necessary?"

My wife and father-in-law were now visibly irked by my probing but still allowed my line of questioning.

"The Children's Hospital of Philadelphia will not make an appointment with you if you do not do this procedure, sir. That's a fact." She smirked, as if she had just beaten me in a game of chess and was waiting for my inevitable compliance.

I looked at the phone on her desk and said, "I'd like to call them."

"Call *who*?" Her eyes narrowed, and her face tightened.

"The Children's Hospital of Philadelphia, " I said slowly enough to imply my insistence.

Nicole tried to intervene, attempting to lighten the tension in the room. "She's a doctor, honey. They know what they're doing. Let's just do it."

Eddie, with the best of intentions, echoed the sentiments of my wife. I looked into Nicole's eyes and saw the sobbing girl from the first night we met. At that moment, I was one hundred percent husband and daddy in the realest sense of the words.

"You don't have to call them. I already know they will not make an appointment without this procedure being done!" The doctor slammed her pen onto the desk.

I looked back at the doctor and with as much determination as I could, knowing that I was being moved by the Holy Spirit and sure of my decision, said, "I insist that I call the children's hospital immediately. May I please use your phone?"

If she could have thrown us out, I assume she would have, but she allowed me to use the phone. Within minutes, I was on the line with the Children's Hospital of Philadelphia's pediatric department, and I explained the situation.

The sweet-sounding receptionist replied, "Oh, sweetheart. You don't have any obligation to do that! We can make an appointment right now. It's no problem at all."

I hung up the phone. The doctor was livid. We awkwardly signed some paperwork, then left her office. Nicole was clearly relieved to have avoided the procedure, and I think a little surprised at how forceful I'd been. Though medical resources online claim the risk is only one out of a hundred, we read about many women who had miscarriages shortly after that procedure. That one could have been our Nikos, and that was too many for me. I only refused it by God's grace. God knew, and he let me know. "My sheep hear my voice, and I know them, and they follow me" (John 10:27 ESV).

Two days later, after a couple sleepless nights, we arrived at the Children's Hospital of Philadelphia. This particular hospital was extremely well-known for their expertise in birth abnormalities, but especially spina bifida. Everyone we talked to told us CHOP was *the* place to go for our son's condition and arguably the best in the country.

The exam room was quiet and dim except for the bright light of the computer monitor, which featured a 4D ultrasound of our son. Our eyes remained glued to that screen for no less than six consecutive hours—which felt like six consecutive days—while they conducted a full day of different types of testing. Nicole lay on the bed in a hospital gown, her beautiful dark hair draped across the pillow, her belly full of life, her hands fidgeting, and her face anxious. We prayed together, talked, and even laughed at times while we watched our baby move around into different positions. The more we watched Nikos, the more hopeful we felt. I had committed to fasting and prayer for two days before the appointment, and I remember how dry my mouth was as we awaited the results.

To our surprise, the first stop after the tests were finished was to see a relocation specialist that would help us relocate to Philadelphia for the next year or so should we choose to continue with the pregnancy.

"Relocate?"

"Oh, yes," the young woman explained. "You'll need to live near the hospital for at least a year."

The implications of that for work and life in general were obviously overwhelming, but we didn't have time to process this before being moved to the next room. We sat at a table with, we'd been told, two of the best neurosurgeons in the United States. The room was small, painted in warm tones, decorated with homey accents, and designed to be comfortable and put people at ease, I assumed. My father-in-law sat with us as the doctors introduced themselves. We were polite as we waited in anticipation for their expert opinion.

"So, unfortunately, your baby has the worst case of spina bifida a child can have. It's called myelomeningocele. There is a hole in his spine, and the nerves are completely exposed. The nerves are being damaged as we speak. The situation is already very bad, but it will be made worse every day until the baby is born."

The heaviness in the room felt like an actual physical pressure weighing down on us and our hopefulness. We remained silent, exchanging a glance that communicated the dread in our hearts.

"We offer an in utero surgery, but unfortunately, you are not eligible for that particular intervention," the female doctor said. "If you decide to carry this baby to full term, there is no telling the damage that will be done. This will result in paralyzation anywhere from the waist down, possibly even above the waist. There's just no telling. It is very likely he will live his life bound to a wheelchair, and there will be multiple brain surgeries throughout his life."

Nicole, Eddie, and I sat completely speechless, all three of us in shock as the already bad news continued to get worse with every additional word. The other doctor pulled a thin plastic tube out of his pocket like a cheap magician.

"This is called a shunt," he said. "If you do decide to bring this pregnancy to term, after birth, we would be surgically implanting this from the baby's brain to the stomach. This tube will continually drain fluid so that pressure does not build in the baby's head. We can't guarantee anything else we've spoken about thus far; however, this surgery in particular will be one hundred percent necessary should you choose to keep this pregnancy. It will be a difficult road, but please understand we do this surgery all the time. Parents do it, but we want you to understand the implications it will have for you and your family."

None of us uttered a word.

"Abortion needs to be discussed, of course. It's an option. We have a clinic across the street that could . . . take care of it for you."

Take care of it, I thought. That wording sounded so familiar. If they could have winked, they would have. *Take care of it*. A strange choice of words, like a discreet offer made by some underworld gangster in a mob movie.

"Unfortunately, per the law in New Jersey, you have only until this coming Tuesday to make your decision. I know this is a lot. Do you have any questions?"

Our son's life was in our hands, and we had four days to decide whether he'd live or die. We had millions of questions, and we asked a few of them, but these doctors didn't have answers for the questions we needed answers to.

We left the hospital, Nicole sobbing in my arms as if Nikos had just been handed a death sentence. Her olive skin was paler than I had ever seen. She doubled over, her tears like waterfalls as she cried out loud.

❀

THREE FULL DAYS AND NIGHTS passed, and we fasted, prayed, and sought counsel from so many people. We just wanted someone to tell us what the right thing to do was. We didn't want Nikos to live a miserable life. We began to focus on fear. How would we handle a situation like this? Were we able? What about Arman? How would it affect him? What about our marriage? Would this destroy us? We talked and we talked, and as we talked, it became more confusing.

My thoughts were incoherent jumbled chaos: life, baby, death, wheelchairs, happy, offspring of the righteous, legacy, faith, birth, defeat, evil, smiles, abortion, belly, do-over, spina bifida, legs, therapy, prayer, spine, future, do not be anxious but, neurological, who, why, how, God, often, later, in the beginning, God created, bloody baby parts on a metal table, satan, brain surgery, thou shalt not, in everything, rest, Jesus, hope, trust, His glory, times of need, in the way you should go, counsel, anxieties, He cares, mercy, doubt, do not be afraid, miracles, pain, only believe, Nikos, victory.

We were out of our minds. We had talked to maybe thirty different people over the span of three days. I'd spent time on the phone with Pastors Bill, Chris, Calvin, and Ara. We spoke with friends, family members, strangers. Some leaned toward abortion; some leaned toward life. People prayed for us and over us. They laid their hands on us, and that made some unbelievers in our life angry. "Enough with all the God stuff," they said. We heard it more than once. No one gave us an answer, or maybe they did and we couldn't hear them. No one else would have to live with the consequences; this was our spiritual fight, and it belonged to no one else.

I was sitting in the car outside my in-laws' house in Belmar, New Jersey, a dead look on my unshaven face, unable or unwilling to speak any more to anyone about anything, when the phone rang. I watched as it vibrated on the center console, displaying a picture of my dad on the screen. I looked at his face carefully as the phone continued to buzz, not wanting to answer. Finally, at the very last second, I picked up. I didn't speak at first.

"Aj? You there, son?"

I had been pretty good about not crying, even though I was dying inside, but my father's voice had always be able to turn me into a five-year-old boy all over again, and I broke. I cried and struggled to explain the details, ending with, "I'm so scared, Dad. I just don't know what to do."

He said only three words, but they were the sweetest and most concise words anyone had spoken to me, and coming from my father, they pierced my heart and comforted me at the same time. "Trust God, son."

Those words echoed through my soul. "Trust in the Lord with all your heart, and do not lean on your own understanding. In all your ways acknowledge Him, and He will make straight your paths" (Proverbs 3:5-6 ESV). I could have been facing anything or anyone at any time, and those words would have been the best advice any father could give. Incredibly simple, incredibly profound.

The fear was watching my own child suffer for a lifetime—brain surgeries, wheelchairs, challenge after challenge. The fear was not knowing what would await us after our decision. So many around us had lightly suggested abortion, reminding us we could always try again, but then I would spend an hour or more at a time staring at my son's face in the sonogram I kept in my pocket to show family members. I spent time alone crying and praying, wanting to make the right decision but not yet able to find the courage.

Later that Sunday night, our pastor, Chris Durkin, came to our house, and after spending some time comforting us, he prayed to God with his hands on Nicole's belly. I remember feeling what felt like waves of joy washing over us, and my son Arman, who was not yet two years old, began to laugh uncontrollably until Pastor Chris left us. It was about 9:00 p.m., and the house was quiet. I had been meaning to call back my good friend and brother Ralph Defilippo. He said something I'll never forget: "No matter what decision you make, we will love you and be here to help you pick up the pieces. After next Tuesday, the weight you feel now will be over because you will have made a decision one way or the other. And that specific pressure will be gone. We've all experienced spiritual victory and spiritual defeat in big and small battles, and you will experience one of those two things, and whether victory or defeat, it will echo throughout the rest of your life."

"Nikos." I said the name over and over again.

His name means *victory*. We chose that name very early in the pregnancy, and we didn't really know why. I hung up the phone that night with the word *victory* playing over and over in my head until I finally went to sleep. I had been praying that God would give me an answer. I wanted a yes or a no. What He gave me was a dream that would serve as both my yes and my no.

In my dream, I walked into a room, where a little boy of about two sat at a rustic wooden table. I had never seen him before, but I knew he was my son. He was eating a meal like they might give out in prison, and I was disgusted by what he'd been given, but he was so grateful for it. He looked up at me with these eyes, these big sweet eyes, and a big smile. He looked at me for love and acceptance. He trusted me and looked at me the way only a child can look at their father, looking to me for everything.

I realized that this was his last meal, though he had absolutely no idea. At the end of this meal, after he took the last bite, I'd have to hand him over to the executioner, but it was completely my choice. I realized this as the sweet little boy kicked his legs under the table, eating his tiny piece of bread and staring at me with a smile.

I woke up crying hysterically. How could I have not seen it before? How could I ever betray my own son? I had never been so sure of anything in my life. Absolutely yes to life. Absolutely no to execution. I got in my work truck and thanked God for the dream, crying out loud, thanking Him with a loud voice. Then I screamed at satan at the top of my lungs, "You can't have him! He doesn't belong to you!"

Just then, I remembered the prayer of two Christian women God had sent to us a day earlier at our most discouraged moment. The mother of one of Nicole's friends and another woman we hadn't known had asked if they could come pray over us and place their hands on my wife's belly. "God, please grant these two wisdom, grace, and mercy. Protect this child, Lord, and do not allow satan to have him. In Jesus's name."

I called Nicole sobbing. "I don't care what he has or how bad it is, we are having this baby." After explaining the dream and knowing God had spoken, the relief washed over both of us like a flood.

If the world had had its way, Nikos would have died in that clinic in Philadelphia. Three months from his due date, his tiny body would have been broken and ripped apart piece by piece by shiny surgical extraction tools, then laid out covered in blood and accounted for by a person in a white coat who didn't care about his name. His tiny head with that new baby smell would have been collapsed and crushed rather than being caressed by his mother's hands. He would have never opened his little eyes to see his mother staring into them while she whispered words of love into his tiny ears. And my wife's body and soul would have been broken as well.

My heart could have shriveled in fear of the unknown and been relinquished to the evil schemes. We could have been deceived by satan himself into executing our own son and calling it "mercy." Our marriage could have been marred by living—or not living—in the perpetual nightmare of a decision we would carry for a lifetime while we lied to ourselves and everyone else about how we'd made the right choice. We could have gone about our lives selfishly, denying the responsibility to which God had called us.

But instead, our faith was only made stronger as we faced every challenge as a family, trusting in God. And then we received one of the two greatest gifts we have ever received when Nikos Edward Kaymakcian was born on October 29, 2018. Dr. Arno Fareed performed surgery on his spine one day later, and then, in the wee hours of the morning, I held my precious son in my arms, so grateful for the dream, so grateful for the surety, so grateful for him and the opportunity to become a daddy a second time, in a deeper way than I could have ever imagined.

My eldest, Arman, wore a tiny shirt that said *Big Brother* while he held his little brother. With a big smile on his little face, he fell in love along with us with the gift of victory.

If the world had had its way, we wouldn't be living this dream of victory, but we are. Thank you, Jesus, we are. I am so proud of my son for facing his challenges head-on and making it look easy. He is one of my greatest heroes, and we will live this dream every day in victory for the rest of our lives. Victory in Jesus, the name above every name.

FINAL ROOM

It's Sure Been Nice Talking to You, Dad

I HAVE WALKED THROUGH HUNDREDS, MAYBE THOU-sands, of different doors throughout my life. I've crossed through doors into rooms that felt like dreams and nightmares. I've seen doorways smashed in by tactical narcotics task forces and opened doors to things a child should never see or hear. I've walked through doors that were locked behind me, where I was sexually abused. I have walked through the filthy doorways of crack houses and abandoned buildings, of motels, of strip clubs, and through doors of mansions and cathedrals. I've walked through doorways of schools, hospitals, therapists, counselors, rehabs, cop cars, jails, funeral homes, Bible studies, museums, churches, parties, celebrations, and reunions. I've walked through the doors of a psychiatric ward, where Jesus Christ saved my life when I was a suicidal heroin addict, and through the doors that led me to my beautiful bride dressed in all white, looking like everything I had ever wanted.

I have walked through doors of beautiful hotel rooms in Athens, Mykonos, and Santorini, where my wife and I enjoyed our honeymoon together. I've walked through doors into rooms I had been waiting to enter since I was a little boy, where my wife gave birth to the two most beautiful boys I have ever seen, and through the doors of our home, where I held them close, whispered to them, and kissed their tiny faces as I wondered what kind of men they would one day become. I've walked through the door to the hospital, where they were supposed to perform brain surgery on my one-month-old, Nikos, and I walked out of that same door with him in my arms after God healed his brain and left the hospital staff in awe, and the surgery was canceled before it had the chance to start.

I have walked through doors in New Jersey, New York, Amsterdam, Mexico, the Caribbean, Greece, Turkey, and many other places, and through the ornate intricately carved wooden doors of the most beautiful kind in Armenia, the place where my father's fathers once walked.

But the door to your house was so unlike any door I had ever walked through in my life, unlike any room I had ever entered. Unlike any door that had ever led me to you or you to me. It stood there in front of me as a rite of passage. I stared at that door painted white, like a whitewashed tomb, unprepared for what would be on the other side.

It was August, and the Florida heat was unbearable. The brightness of the sun dimmed as I walked inside that day. My eyes struggled to acclimate to the darkness. Familiar pictures of us all and the lingering scent of a million cigarettes smoked back-to-back in that tiny house led me along as I made my way back to you.

I walked into your room and said, "Dad, I'm here!" as if I had been in a race to get to you—or as if you had been counting down to the moment I arrived.

I knew you were waiting for me, but you said nothing—not "Hey, buddy," or "*Inch goo nes, yavrik?*" *What's goin' on, little one?* or "Oh, thought you forgot about your old dad," in that sarcastic tone that was meant to mean *I've missed you so much, and I'm so glad you're here.*

I wanted to hug you like you'd hugged me after I went through that window when I was a kid, and like we had so many times before. But not this time. Your silence was a different kind of silence, beyond silent, unending silence, the kind of silence that's so quiet it sounds like a noise, the kind that filled my heart with a terror and sadness I had never felt before.

I hated the way your mouth was open a little, exposing the cracked and missing teeth you had worked so hard to hide from me the last few years whenever I made a joke. I miss your smile, Dad—the one full of teeth, the one you made when I needed everything to be okay, the one accompanied by a wink.

I put my ear to your chest, which was like a skeleton's, with nothing but a thin layer of flesh over top it, and I didn't hear your heartbeat, the one I used to hear while we napped on the first floor in the room right next to the stairs, the same room you had a dream in that you'd won the lottery and stashed the money under the mattress, only to wake up broke. When I was a little boy and you were tired from work, all I wanted to do was wake you up to play. I hated when you wouldn't wake up back then.

The finality of your absence was a presence. Your eyes, the ones that looked like they belonged to a young boy, were still clear, and I thought maybe, just maybe, you could still hear me when I held your hands and told you I was sorry. And I was, I am, so sorry. I'm sorry. I'm sorry I didn't get there sooner and that I couldn't have done more for you, Dad. So sorry that life was so hard for you. Sorry that you struggled so much for so long. Sorry life ended like this.

I'm sorry I gave you that bag of heroin all those years ago when I was a desperate restless stupid kid, only focused on myself, not thinking about how it would affect you. I'm sorry I believed that maybe you were right, that you were stronger than me, that it was just my particular brand of weakness that made me powerless to the drug from a beautiful sinister-looking field of poppy flowers that so many men have succumbed to.

As I knelt at your bedside, I thought about whoever it was that had sold you the dope and methamphetamine you mixed together, causing the massive stroke that left your body and brain so broken. I wonder what he spent the money on—maybe some jewelry or clothes like I used to when I sold drugs, wishing someone would love me, accept me, respect me, wanting to hide from who I really was. Maybe he spent it on drugs. Maybe he'd overdosed and was lying dead somewhere. Maybe he was in prison. Or maybe Jesus had saved him too, and he was out telling someone about all the good the Lord had done in transforming his life, like me.

I wonder what it was like to live every day with the consequences of that one decision as you limped the rest of your way through life, what it must have been like to have dreams that you were running fast like you used to when I was little, only to wake up bound to the bed. I miss the conversations we used to have before the stroke affected your speech. I miss the closeness we had before I was saved and everything in my life changed. I miss . . . you.

It doesn't matter, I guess. You're gone now, and there's nothing I can do to bring you back. But I won't remember you that way, wasted away, just another victim of the worst drug epidemic America has ever seen, your legs like sticks under the hospital gown you died in, a look of mild shock on your face.

I watched as your eyes slowly became cloudy as life fled them.

The scar was still there as I drenched your hand with tears. The scar wasn't from a carpet iron; it was from a dark time following your brother Pete's suicide after he found out you were with his wife, Sandy, the girl you fell in love with first—a complicated situation that no one would ever quite understand. You burned five cigarettes down to the filter on top of your hand while you were drunk and mourning what had happened. You did it to feel something other than the guilt, leaving behind third-degree burns, not very different from how I cut myself as a kid. Your scar, which was a lifelong reminder of your guilt and regret, had washed out and now blended together with mine. That scar on your hand that always told me stories about you has become a scar in my life that tells me stories about me, stories I might have rather not known.

I'm sure about that though, Dad. I won't remember you like that. I'd much rather remember sitting on your shoulders as you walked across the field toward Convention Hall in Asbury Park when the grass got too tough for my tiny feet. You said, "You gotta have karate feet," as you hoisted me up. I'm not a kid anymore; I'm a man with kids on my shoulders, and your feet can't bear any of my pain. I'll have to walk the rest of this life without you, moving closer and closer to my own ending with every passing day, knowing that if you did it, I will be able to do it too. The world was a beautiful place on top of your shoulders, when the ocean breeze breathed toward us, the Berkeley-Carteret, where your brother shot himself, in plain sight—a reminder of your painful past, but nothing more than a castle to me.

No more pain now. It's all a million miles away, Dad.

I will choose to live the rest of my life atop the shoulders of giants. The view is much clearer on top of hundreds of men traced all the way back to Noah's son Japheth, who you told me as a kid was the first of all Armenians. Every one of them stands in a long line, waiting to take their turn among each generation and then stepping off the cliff into eternity. I guess I'm up. It's my turn now, and one day, it will be my sons' turn..

I will choose to remember the days like the one when I cut half my finger off with a carpet knife. I panicked as my finger gushed bright red. You yelled at me to calm down and sprinkled tobacco from your cigarette on the gash, then duct taped it back together. Like some kind of a magician, you told me tobacco used to be used as an antiseptic and to stop bleeding—one of those old-world Armenian remedies that seemed like nonsense until I took the duct tape off a week later and found my finger completely healed. How did you know this stuff? I remember wondering. How was I supposed to learn how to be a man like you were? I took cold showers in the hotel some mornings, wondering why it was so much easier for you than me. Same as I wondered how you slept on the floor as if it were a cloud.

I still felt like a kid on those afternoons when we left work and sat at Vic's in Bradley Beach. At a table by the bar between the old wooden walls, we had a large sausage-and-pepper pizza and cold beers, hot cups of minestrone, and small loaves of bread. We talked about life, and that booth became like a confessional for both of us, and how we would laugh together on a rainy afternoon . . . What I wouldn't give for that now, Dad.

I remember those cold winters when we wrestled around the lobby of the hotel, the fireplaces glaring. I basked in the warmth of your love as we battled for the hat you said had "the power." I swung wildly like a little bull. I couldn't have hurt you then, but I wonder how it hurt on the days I didn't call you back right away. The stroke had made your words difficult to understand, and sometimes it was hard for me to answer the phone. It was hard to deal with the state heroin had left you in, and I was busy piecing my life together, raising my sons, loving my wife. I'm sorry if I hurt you. I tried to understand. I tried to pray with you. I tried to hear you, to listen to you. Now you're gone, and this is just an empty house, the only one you lived in that I don't know intimately.

I'm sorry I didn't get there sooner. I wanted to be with you in those last moments. I hope you weren't scared. I hope it wasn't too painful as you quietly left everything you've ever known. Knowing that you faced death makes me less afraid of facing it myself, if that's any consolation, Pop. Jesus said that if your right arm causes you to sin, you should cut it off, or your right eye, pluck it out. It's better you enter the Kingdom of Heaven maimed than go to hell bodily sound. I'm grateful for the condition the stroke left you in, not because of the pain it brought with it, but because of the hope and peace you found in Jesus. God has His ways, doesn't He, Bub? We would have never stopped, never turned, never repented if not for God's grace in our lives. You were right all those times you told me to trust God. I'm grateful for the father you were, and not only for the good things, but for the bad ones too. I learned from them both. Now it's my turn to be a father, to teach my sons to trust God.

It was so hard to sleep in your house that night after the police came and the paramedics took your body. Your empty Velcro shoes and a cane sat next to your bed, killing me inside. Pictures of happier times stretched across your walls. My sinus infection raged, and the smell of smoke was like torture. You should know that your little dog, who you had lovingly named Jordy Jordanian, wouldn't leave my side all night. It was nice to have each other. I petted him, and he kept me company. That was the agreement we settled on, and I think it was fair.

The next few days were strange. I spent time with your little brother, who took me to the pawnshop where one of your rings was—the square diamond one I'd ask you to borrow, and you'd say to me, "Aj, what do you think that ring is gonna do for you?" After that, we bought a few groceries and brought them back to the house. I'd brought *sujuk*, Armenian dried sausage, for you from New Jersey, which I ate with some cheap feta from the grocery store without you. It didn't taste anything like those lunches we used to have together on summer afternoons on the hotel porch when Grandpa would come from New York with *sujuk* and *basturma*, mortadella with pistachios, and feta cheese he would rinse in cold water to lessen the salt, along with the softest freshest bread I ever had. The bread was stale in Florida, the *sujuk* was bland, and you weren't there to share it with.

So many people called to tell me they were sorry that you'd died, and I appreciated the calls, but honestly, I just wanted to be left alone. After Raphi and Amanda came, we went to meet Aunt Mari at the airport. She got us a hotel room that night, and I made an appointment with the funeral home the next day. We sat in the room, and I felt guilty we didn't have more money to ship your body back to New Jersey. We settled on cremation and arranged to have your ashes shipped to us. Raphi and I talked about what kind of containers we might keep you in. I decided to buy an antique Palais De Versailles white porcelain lion-shaped trinket box with Armenian flag colors bordering the bottom, like one of those rare treasures we might have bought at the Collingwood Auction.

Drugs will always be your mouth open wide with cracked teeth, overgrown hair, your skeleton covered with thin skin dressed in a hospital gown that you wore like burial clothes, and a pair of cloudy eyes void of the glow they once had when you'd look at me, my daddy, the one who held me in his arms. A living corpse that had finally breathed his last breath, a vision that will haunt me until the day I die. That is what drugs will be to me. And when I think of them, I'll think of you. I'll think of us, and I'll continue to mourn.

I SAT IN THE LIVING room of my house—the one you never got to see—and stared at the picture of you and me with our faces pressed together, the gentleness in your eyes reminding me of when we were best friends. My kids played wildly, laughing and play fighting, making noise I didn't hear while I struggled to make sense of all that had happened.

"Do you miss your daddy?" Arman asked. Nikos stood on the other side of me.

"Yeah, buddy. I really do."

"I understand, Daddy," he said, the innocence of his little voice comforting me.

"Hey, Dad?" Nikos asked.

"Yes, *yavrik*?"

"Are you growing a beard on your face?"

"I guess I am, buddy."

"I like your mustache, Dad," Arman said.

"You do?"

"Yeah, we like it, Dad," said Nikos.

Arman asked, "Will I have a mustache when I grow up?"

"Sure you will, son. You'll have one when you grow up. A perfect one," I assured him.

I held both of them tight in my arms with their faces pressed against my shoulders.

"I want to be just like you, Dad," Arman whispered.

"Me too, Dad!" Nikos said, and a tear fell from my eye.

"You will, guys. Believe me, you will."

Thank you so much for reading He Calls Me Redeemed. Please scan QR code to review. I would appreciate it so much. God bless you.
-AK

I want to partner with your church, school, hospital, rehabilitation facility, or correctional institution. Please inquire about bulk sales, television / radio/ podcast appearances, or speaking engagements at Akaymakcian@gmail.com

CALL TO ACTION

I WOULD LIKE TO THANK YOU FROM THE BOTTOM OF my heart for taking the time to read what I've written. If at any time during this book you said to yourself, "I've never struggled with drugs or alcohol or sexual abuse, so this book isn't meant for me," please understand this book is not about drugs or alcohol or childhood sex abuse, nor was it ever meant to be. Drug addiction, as well as sexual abuse, are just symptoms. You or someone you know are experiencing now, have experienced in the past, or will experience some version of these or other symptoms in the future. They are symptoms of a darkness in need of a diagnosis that we all, as human beings, need to hear and understand if we ever hope to rise above.

That diagnosis is sin.

I wish people didn't believe the ridiculous caricatures the world makes Christians out to be. I wish people could understand we call out sin not because we think we are better, but because before Jesus, we were worse off. I wish they knew our hearts and that the love we have fuels us to have difficult, sometimes even dangerous conversations. I wish they knew Jesus loves sinners and wants to save them and that His true followers share the same sentiment.

As I sit here this morning in 2023, the world looks like it's on fire. It seems as though we are living through so much of what Jesus warned about the end times. Global pandemics, mass vaccination, food shortages, what appears to be by many experts an imminent global economic collapse, massive earthquakes, wars and rumors of wars, nations rising against nations, full-scale military invasions of sovereign countries and nuclear threats, geopolitical and financial exploitation of those invasions, a genocide of Artsakh Armenians in plain sight, terrorism. Symptoms.

So-called "artificial intelligence" is, at the time of this publication, beginning to take the world by storm and paving the way for global deception and surveillance, the likes of which we have not yet seen and can't possibly understand. In the United States more specifically, with the ridiculous politically hyperpolarized climate we find ourselves in, the media pushes narratives of constant conflict between races and ethnicities and battles between the sexes.

There is a full-scale assault on children by way of indoctrination through the public school system that continues into universities, raising generations of people who've completely bought into ideologies that promote and celebrate the breakdown of the family as we know it. We see overt evil and extraordinarily inappropriate behavior, such as scantily clad drag queens being invited by political figures, teachers, and so-called "leaders" to read to small children in public schools, government buildings, and libraries, as well as parents bringing their own children to sexually perverse events and even encouraging some confused children as young as ten years old to perform onstage like strippers while dollar bills are thrown amidst a roar of cheers from adults who look on.

I can't even believe I'm writing this, because just a few short years ago, this behavior would have been an impossibility. When Christians warned people this was coming, they were laughed at and mocked. However, it is now plain to see that the sexualization of our children is being normalized and becoming mainstream as we speak. I fear the push for legal pedophilia will be a reality in the coming years. Already, there are groups and organizations who suggest that MAP, or "minor-attracted person," would be a more sympathetic and politically correct term to use than *pedophile*, and these groups advocate for their inclusion in the LGBTQ community.

As a person who has suffered the consequences of childhood sexual abuse, that is a petrifying notion. Parents across the country unwittingly offer their own children on the altar of satan himself, whether they understand it or not, when they sexualize and mutilate them by way of surgical sex changes and chemical castration during adolescence. Many physicians and mental health experts have voiced their concern over the lack of ability to openly question the legitimacy behind these requests. Through virtue signaling, in return for the precious sacrifice of their babies, they receive applause and accolades from the world system, more money, more influence, more power, and more fame.

Famous pop stars parade onstage dressed as satan surrounded by demonic imagery and symbolism at major award shows, while thousands of adoring fans cheer for them. Brave production company Angel Studios and producer Eduardo Verástegui, through their groundbreaking film *Sound of Freedom*, have shined a light on human trafficking, which is a global horror story raking in an estimated whopping $150 billion annually, as per *Forbes Magazine*, among many other sources. Child sexual abuse is rampant. Pornography pulls in $14 billion annually, according to *Forbes Magazine*, gripping both men and women. Many of the adult film stars featured in these movies suffer from sexually transmitted diseases and mental health issues, and sadly, many have taken their own lives. As social media pressures continue to ramp up, young girls are undergoing cosmetic surgeries and objectifying themselves in hopes of being accepted. Many women are part of a site called OnlyFans, where users pay lots of money for explicit images and videos that will one day haunt the women's children, and many of those children will no doubt be the victims of bullying and suicidal ideation. Adultery, divorce, broken homes, and displaced children are at an all-time high. Suicide rates are skyrocketing among confused teenagers, as well as adults, who are inundated with drugs, both illegal and prescribed, while large pharmaceutical companies rake in billions of dollars. Fentanyl from China has poured into our country by the ton through Mexico and has killed over 100,000 people in 2022 alone, and it's barely covered in the media.

Symptoms.

And what about those lives that are ended before they even begin? 73,000,000. Yup, that's six zeros. 73,000,000 abortions are performed annually, per the World Health Organization. That's 73,000,000 distinct people, helpless babies who will never get a chance at life.

All of this, and I haven't even mentioned a plethora of other issues we face, which I could easily write another book about. The bottom line is, people are lost, confused, distracted, weighed down, exhausted, and inundated by the Godless culture they find themselves in. Please hear me. I don't say these things to insult any particular group of people. I'm only stating the facts as I see them from my vantage point according to my biblical worldview. We are now living in a world where not only is there no clear right or wrong, good or bad, up or down, but the perception is that wrong *is* right, bad *is* good, and down *is* up. Morality has been hijacked and made subjective, and as our society veers further and further away from our Judeo-Christian roots, the more confused and wicked and polarized we will become.

This book is about the "good news" the message of the gospel, Jesus Christ is the answer for every problem. It is for young people confused about their sexuality and for those who think about suicide every day. It's for the husband and wife going through a painful divorce, for all the young parents, and for those who've just received a devastating diagnosis for their unborn son or daughter or find themselves in a precarious financial situation and are considering abortion. It's for those who've just lost someone who meant everything to them and for the drug addict or alcoholic who sees no possible way out. It's for the young and the old, for the lonely and the lost, as well as those who are surrounded by friends and think they have it all figured out. For the influencer or the entrepreneur, for the rich and the poor, for the weak and the strong. For the churchgoer, for the atheist and the agnostic, for the new age people, for the lovers of many faiths, and for those who refer to themselves as spiritual. For the beautiful and the ugly.

For the person who's had what anyone would call a perfect life and considers themselves self-sufficient, hear me when I say there is no self-sufficiency without Jesus. You are wholly insufficient, and you likely feel it in your soul every day. Something is missing.

These are all symptoms, and here is the diagnosis: we are sinners. This book is for sinners, and that means it's for everyone. And when we breathe our final breath, we will face God and be judged for our sin. Jesus stepped into time and space, into human history, and took the form of an infant born of a virgin. God in the flesh, just like you and me. He lived a sinless life, was tortured and crucified, died, was resurrected, and walked out of His own grave three days later.

To have the opportunity to escape the wrath that is coming on the whole world, you must surrender. Whoever you are, wherever you are, and whatever you've done, there is hope for you in Jesus Christ. Forgiveness for you, rest for you, in Jesus Christ. You can be forgiven and have peace with God today right here as you read this, through Jesus if you will believe in your heart and confess with your mouth that He is Lord, and that He is who He says He is. He will come into your heart and change your life for all eternity. The consequences of your surrender to Jesus will be monumental, as they were and are for me, as you've read in this book. Everything—and I do mean everything—in your life will become new: family, marriage, children, relationships, work, finance, love, sexuality. Your life will not be perfect—mine sure isn't—but you will live a blessed life and have peace even in the storms, and when you go through difficulties, you will have Jesus to guide you through them.

I would love if you would share this book with others and leave honest reviews on Amazon, which I'll leave a link for in the back of this book. I'd be so grateful for that. I'd love if you would visit my website, www.ArmanKaymakcian.com, reach out to me through social media, and keep an eye out for future projects. I'd love to connect with you and hear your feedback. But more than all that, my hope and my prayer and what I'd love most is if you would honestly examine your life and your heart and ask yourself the hard questions. I'd love it if you would hear the Gospel—the good news—through my book, get alone with God, and have a moment like I did all those years ago when I was hopeless and ready to give up on life.

I hope you know that whoever you are and whatever you've done or are currently doing, Jesus loves you and wants to come into your life like He came into mine. "For God did not send his Son into the world to condemn the world, but to save the world through him" (John 3:17 NIV). I would love if that one honest vulnerable moment you have with Jesus, the creator and sustainer of all things, changed your life forever. I would love it if you brought all your pain and your mess to Him, because He cares for you. I'd love for you to be delivered and free from the fear of death and the exhaustion of fighting against God and feeling the weight and consequences of the sins you've committed, that you'd be transformed by grace through faith in Jesus Christ and have new life in Him.

I'd love it if my book helped you. That's why I wrote it. In the words of Samuel Rutherford, "My witness is above; your heaven would be two heavens to me, and the salvation of you all as two salvations to me." I'd love it if you turned toward God, turned away from evil, and were saved, and if my story was somehow a part of your story, I'd love that too. And I'd love to see you one day and break bread with you in heaven a million miles away from pain, from tears, from fears, and from loss. That is my prayer, in Jesus's name, amen.

Then I saw "a new heaven and a new earth," for the first heaven and the first earth had passed away, and there was no longer any sea. I saw the Holy City, the new Jerusalem, coming down out of heaven from God, prepared as a bride beautifully dressed for her husband. And I heard a loud voice from the throne saying, "Look! God's dwelling place is now among the people, and he will dwell with them. They will be his people, and God himself will be with them and be their God. 'He will wipe every tear from their eyes. There will be no more death' or mourning or crying or pain, for the old order of things has passed away."

He who was seated on the throne said, "I am making everything new!"

Revelation 21:1-5 New International Version

ACKNOWLEDGMENTS

First and foremost, I thank God for saving me and transforming my life, for the sacrifice He made on the cross, and for making the richness of His grace and mercy available to someone who was as lost as I once was. There has been no one else who has done for me what Jesus has done. I could have never written this book without His inspiration and leading.

To Nicole, my lovely wife, my beautiful bride, the love of my life, and my best friend. Thank you for the endless sacrifices you've made for our family and for the endless moments of happiness we've shared together. You have been light for me on many cloudy days. Proverbs 18:22 says, "He who finds a wife finds a good thing and obtains favor from the Lord." You have been a good thing for me. I love you with all my heart and soul, and I couldn't have done it without you.

To my sons, Arman and Nikos. I cannot express in words the joy and blessings you have brought into my life.

I am forever grateful for your love. As I've said, you are my crowning achievements. Thank you for your encouragement.

To my dog, Nemo, for all those cold early mornings I sat down to write and you curled up next to me and stared at me as if you understood that what I was attempting to do was the most difficult thing I had ever done.

To my brother, Raphi, for endless conversations about this book when no one else would listen and for being not only my younger brother, but a friend and brother in Christ with incredible strength that I admire and will forever appreciate. And to his incredible wife, my sister-in-law, Amanda. You are one of the most loving, kindhearted, and beautiful people I have ever met.

To my sister, Michele, for pancakes early in the morning and for teaching me to drive way earlier than I should have been behind the wheel, and to my niece, Precious, and her father, Mike Tulley.

To my mother, Tobe. You put up with copious amounts of selfishness and stupidity at the worst times of my life and loved me anyway. For the sacrifices you made during my youth, for ziti with light sauce from Palumbo's and for 11:00 p.m. talks at our kitchen table. For all the double shifts and difficult times, thank you.

To my stepfather, Artie, for doing your best to help me become a man in the midst of all my chaos, for trying to teach me to lift weights, and for your attempt at discipline. For late-night pay-per-view events and new movies on the cable box on Airsdale Avenue. And to his children, Robert and McKenna, for many afternoons we played together in the yard and for scary movies and sleepovers.

To my father, Manuk, for showing me how to be a man in ways I only fully understood after he was gone. For his creativity, love, affection, unorthodox way of living life, and incredible toughness.

To my stepmother, Karen, for afternoons on the hotel porch where you taught me to crochet, and for early-morning toast with Nutella, or peanut butter and tea.

To my grandfather Tony, for being a second father to me, for endless afternoons enjoying art and literature, for coffee and chocolate milk and cinnamon rolls from Freedman's Bakery in the Seaview Square Mall, for good conversation, and for his genuine heart and love for me.

To my grandma Betty, for afternoons when I stayed home sick at her house with a bell and small packages of Lorna Doone cookies by my side.

To my little cousins, Manny and Petey, for Sunday mornings on our way to St. Stepanos Armenian Apostolic Church and for the nonstop comedy. And to my beautiful first cousin once removed, baby Manuk, and his beautiful mother, Courtney, for the strength and joy I see in you both.

To my eldest cousin, Martina, for bowls of cereal in adjoining rooms on the second floor of the Armenian Royal Hotel or apartments in Queens, New York, with shelves of glass statues we weren't able to touch.

To my uncles Jirayir and Arax and their wives, Lisa and Jutta, for walking with me to Sixth Avenue beach, watching wrestling for hours, play fighting with me, waiting patiently for me as a toddler to pick out not one, but two candies from the 7-Eleven on Main Street, and carrying me on your shoulders. I'll never forget it.

To my cousins Rob and Peter and their wives, Aphroditi (Aph) and Marianne, and their children, Nola and Tess, for the love and laughter, for unmatched hospitality, for hiking, and for incredible memories visiting my family's church in Montreal.

To my grandparents, Arman and Elli, for cozy afternoons in their apartment on Sixth Avenue, for classical music, Persian rugs, beautifully arrayed cold cuts, good wine, Baci chocolates, and insightful conversations.

To my maternal grandmother, Mari. Though we never got a chance to meet, I'm grateful for the warmth and love my father told me about in stories of you and for the untold stories I've imagined in my mind's eye.

To Aunt Mari and Uncle Danny, for your love and for sending me books from the time I was young. I honestly believe I never would have written this book if it weren't for you. For taking me to the American Museum of Natural History in Manhattan as a child, which I still remember thirty-five years later. For your constant encouragement and seemingly endless compliments, and for always seeing my potential, thank you.

To my father-in-law, Eddie, for your kindness and generosity and for trusting me with your daughter despite knowing my past. And to my mother-in-law, Joanne, for all of your hard work and dedication to your family, and for countless delicious holiday meals, for your constant encouragement and compliments and spirit. Both of you have loved me and welcomed me like a son, and I'm grateful for you.

To my brother-in-law Eddie Jr., for your heart of gold and the direct way in which you approach life. And to my sister-in-law Kasey, for your kindness and never-ending generosity and for helping me order gifts for my wife. And for your famous buffalo chicken dip no one can seem to replicate.

To my sister-in-law Taylor, for your love and your many talents and also for helping me find gifts for my wife when I'm out of ideas. And to my brother-in-law Mike, for your kindness and help in times of need and for your family's warmth and hospitality.

To Aunt Ellen, for your love and generosity, for the interest and attention you always show to Arman and Nikos, and for your encouragement and compliments and endless warm afternoons in Vic's where you help me remember my dad.

To Aunt Diane and her sons, Mikey, John, and Stevie, and their wives and girlfriends, Christine, Cathryn, and Liz, and their children, McKenzie and little Johnny, for your warmth and always welcoming me as family.

To Uncle Nicky, for your love and conversations and for the afternoons you spent fixing our cars.

To Uncle John and his wife, Erin, and their children, Hudson and Payton, for all of your love and support and the unbelievable hospitality your family has always shown us.

Thanks to Pastor Bill Beckelman, Pastor Chris Durkin, Pastor Calvin Sagherian, and Pastor Jacob Navey and their families, for your encouragement and words of wisdom at some of the most difficult times in my life as well as the most joyful, and for your unending dedication to the spiritual growth of my own family as well as the entire family of God.

To my brothers and sisters in Christ, who have been an oasis in the desert that is this fallen world. So many are your names and so countless are the ways in which you've encouraged me, loved me, and prayed for me and my family. If I were to write a sentence for each one of you, this book would contain many, many more chapters. You know who you are, and I'm so grateful for you.

To my little brother in Christ, Jack Cerulo, for suggesting I write this book, for wishing I were included in the list of "the great men in Christian history," for your love for the church, talent in music (among many other things), for your pure heart and longing for God, and for your boldness and tenacity.

To everyone who took the time to read an advanced copy of the book and give me their honest feedback, especially my good friend and brother Tom Rivenburg, who carefully dissected the book and acted as an unofficial editor.

I'd like to also say a special thank-you to David Kherdian, for your contribution to Armenian literature, the many letters and phone calls we shared, your encouragement as a fellow writer, writing a blurb for my debut memoir, and for allowing me to be a part of your legacy.

To my editors, Chelsea and Natalia at Enchanted Ink Publishing. I'm incredibly grateful for the many beautiful carefully crafted words of encouragement as well as the direct and honest way you pointed out things I would have never even considered about my own writing. Thank you for elevating my project in such a profound and professional way.

And to those I have not mentioned by name, please do not feel left out. There are hundreds and hundreds of people who have touched my life and paved the way for the writing of this story. You've taught me many lessons, and I'm grateful to you as well.

I am honored and humbled.

Stay Connected! Please scan QR code to visit my website. Where you can follow me on social media, leave me prayer requests, sign up for my newsletter, and stay updated on future publications, special events, appearances, and book signings.

SCAN TO STAY CONNECTED

WWW.ARMANKAYMAKCIAN.COM

I want to partner with your church, school, hospital, rehabilitation facility, or correctional institution. Please inquire about bulk sales, television / radio/ podcast appearances, or speaking engagements at Akaymakcian@gmail.com

ARMAN KAYMAKCIAN

is an Armenian-American author and poet. He was born in New Jersey in the 1980s. He grew up living between his Italian family on his mother's side in Long Branch and his Armenian family in the historic town of Asbury Park. His life journey inspired him to begin writing. As a promise to himself, his first major literary work is a product of his redemption in life through Jesus Christ. Arman writes from the perspective of an Armenian American, yet his story is very much American. His vast life experiences allow him to explore themes such as culture, crime, death, and spirituality with authenticity. *He Calls Me Redeemed* is his debut memoir.

WWW.ARMANKAYMAKCIAN.COM